Mary Slessor

The Barefoot Missionary

ELIZABETH ROBERTSON

NMS Publishing Limited

Published by NMS Publishing Limited
National Museums of Scotland, Chambers Street, Edinburgh EH1 1JF

Series editor: Iseabail Macleod

ISBN 1-901663-50-7

Other titles available in the Scots' Lives series:

The Gentle Lochiel	*Miss Cranston*
Elsie Inglis	*Mungo Park*
The Scottish Suffragettes	

Forthcoming titles:

Reginald Johnston	*Mary of Guise*
Twa Tribes	

British Library Cataloguing in Publication Data
 A catalogue record of this book
 is available from the British Library.

Typeset in 11/13 pt Baskerville.
Internal design layout by NMS Publishing Limited.
Cover concept by Mark Blackadder. Adapted by Cara Shanley.
Cover and art section repro by Marshall Thomson Digital Communication.
Printed and bound in the United Kingdom by Bell & Bain Ltd, Glasgow.

Acknowledgements

I WISH to express my gratitude to the following for helping to make my research pleasurable and rewarding:

Ian Flett, Dundee City Archivist; the Local Studies Department of Dundee Central Library; the McManus Galleries, Dundee; Rev. Professor Kenneth Ross, General Secretary of the Church of Scotland Board of World Mission; Dr Louise A Yeoman, Manuscript Department of the National Library of Scotland.

I am especially indebted to Iseabail Macleod for her encouragement throughout, and to Helen Kemp and Lesley Taylor of NMS Publishing, where Cara Shanley deserves a special mention for her enthusiasm and unfailing helpfulness. Thanks are also due to my former local Librarian, Wendy Sharp, who searched for out of print books with patience and resourcefulness, and Zena Burgess, a former Calabar missionary, whose knowledge and experience of the area were invaluable. I must also thank my personal cartographer, Stuart Ogg, and electronic wizards John Harris and Alan Robertson – as well as the aspiring one, Alex Robertson – who succeeded in rescuing my manuscript from cyber space and me from despair. Finally I wish to record my appreciation of the uniquely valuable contribution of Francis Ita Udom, who knows Mary Slessor country better than most.

Elizabeth Robertson

Picture Acknowledgements

The illustrations in the art section of this book are courtesy of Dundee City Council, Arts and Heritage Department. The picture of Francis Ita Udom was kindly loaned by Francis.

Cover illustrations: *front* – Mary Slessor on a trip to Scotland in 1898 with some of the children she adopted, photo courtesy of Dundee City Council, Arts and Heritage Department; *back* – the Mary Slessor window, McManus Galleries, Dundee; Mary in Calabar, both courtesy of Dundee City Council, Arts and Heritage Department; Calabar ceremonial paddles believed to have been a gift to Mary from King Eyo VII. They were given to Thomas Filler RN by a Presbyterian Church in Calabar with which he was associated during 1923, photograph by courtesy of Catherine Filler.

Contents

The area of Nigeria where Mary Slessor worked between 1876 and 1915.
(Map by courtesy of Stuart Ogg.)

Introduction

ONCE every Sunday School child in the land knew of Mary Slessor of Calabar. Yet many people today, unfamiliar with her history, may wonder why she was chosen to be the first woman depicted on a Scottish banknote. It was to honour one of the most remarkable Scotswomen of her generation.

Calabar, in Southern Nigeria, had been a principal slaving port since the beginning of the eighteenth century. Its trade devastated the Efik tribes, who lost their sons in the prime of manhood, had their morality debased and their culture destroyed. They were believed to have come to the coast almost two centuries before from the Ibibio territory, and made their living from fishing, trading their catches for palm oil and vegetables with tribes inland. In his book, *The Expendable Mary Slessor* (Edinburgh 1980), James Buchan tells us:

> *The tribes all traded with one another. Some were farmers, some fishermen, some made canoes, some pottery, and some wove raffia cloth, while a tribe of travelling blacksmiths did metal work ... tribes like the Efik owned few, if any, domestic slaves. It was this simple way of life that the slave trade destroyed.*

In 1833 a well-known explorer, MacGregor Laird, maintained that Calabar was the most uncivilised part of Africa he had ever visited. However, nine years later, its two ruling chiefs were persuaded by the British, in return for compensation, to sign a final treaty to stop exporting slaves. Although William Wilberforce had put an end to the British slave traffic in 1807, the French and Portuguese still continued the practice, and Cuba and Brazil exported 135,000 slaves from the Guinea Coast in 1836 alone. Now both chiefs were looking for other ways of employing their surplus manpower and they recognised that education was the key to achieving their aim. They were also pro-British, and had no wish to be annexed by the French or Portuguese, whose tentacles were spreading throughout the Guinea Coast. Discovering that missionaries of the United Secession Church who were working in Jamaica were interested in going to Calabar, the chiefs pursued the matter through captains of trading vessels who acted as mediators. They offered land and protection in return for 'Book' (education) and were willing to accept the white God as part of the deal.

Negotiations took three years to complete, through slowness in communication and through opposition from the Scottish Missionary Society which was familiar with the Niger coast's reputation as one of the deadliest places on earth. Men went to such places 'as though condemned', and some were known to take their coffins with them. However, permission was finally given and the Rev. Hope Waddell set out in 1846 with a small group of fellow missionaries, including Christian ex-slaves originating from Calabar who had been given assurance that they would have equal protection.

Today many people think that the ideologies of early missionaries were politically incorrect, and that it was arrogance on their part to attempt to change the ancient customs and beliefs of another culture. However, the customs around Calabar had previously become distorted and beliefs reduced to a cruel travesty: that seemed reason enough for Waddell and his party to go there with their Gospel of love. They went in a true spirit of humility, wishing to atone for the evils perpetrated by the slavers.

In time the mission became well established, and its influence was so effective that the worst tribal practices ceased within the immediate area, with a measure of stability taking over. Then Mary Slessor, fiery and unpredictable, arrived 30 years after the establishment of the mission to change the whole face of missionary endeavour.

There have been many missionaries as dedicated, pursuing their shining aspirations with quiet steadfastness, but it was Mary who captured the public imagination. In that less secular age, people of all denominations (and none) responded to the extraordinary courage and commitment of this lone Scotswoman who took Christianity where no European had gone before. Admiration reached heights which would have destined her for sainthood, had she not been a thoroughgoing Presbyterian. 'Mariolatry', one wit called it at the time. Yet another who knew her well later protested that 'she was nae sae holy', a comment with which Mary would be the first to agree. Brought up within the strictures of the United Presbyterian Church (which the United Secession Church became part of in 1847), her startling blend of orthodoxy and unconventionality would become more apparent with time, along with her remarkable ability to reach into the Nigerian mind. Throughout, she channelled the force of her quick mind and considerable determination into improving the lot of the Africans, and as *Eka Kpukpro Owo* (the Mother of the Peoples) she would become venerated over hundreds of miles.

Yet one of her most important achievements has often been overlooked. A woman ahead of her time, although her radical methods sometimes provoked criticism, she became a much needed bridge-builder during the inflammatory period of Southern Nigeria's transition to a British Protectorate. Perhaps the key to her success lies in her well-thumbed Bible, still preserved in Dundee. Above a passage referring to God's secure protection, she has boldly written: 'God and one, are always a majority.' Such a belief, coupled with the uncompromising fearlessness and tenacity which characterised the whole of her life, has ensured Mary Slessor's place in history.

Chapter 1
Early Days in Dundee

MARY Mitchell Slessor was born in 1848 in Aberdeen, where her early memories included playing at missionaries with her brother Robert, who already had aspirations in that direction. Always cast as a dark-skinned heathen, she would wait nearly 30 years to play the leading role. Through their mother and the United Presbyterian Church they knew the plot inside out, but were unaware of a darker one unfolding. Their father, Robert Slessor, a shoemaker and 'a decent enough man when sober', was losing his battle against the alcoholism that cost him his job, forcing the family to the breadline and his wife to the verge of despair. The family's misery was compounded when Mary's brother Robert died unexpectedly from tuberculosis.

In 1859 they were forced to move to Dundee where, like ten thousand others, they lived in a one-roomed home known as a single end. The city's sudden expansion owed much to the introduction of power-driven looms in the new textile mills that offered plenty of work – especially for women and children, who provided cheap labour. So Mary at the age of eleven became a 'half-timer' with Baxter Brothers, working five hours each day and for the rest of it attending a school provided by the mills. Later she said, 'At that time I was wee and thin and not very strong'. Ever present was the fear of consumption, which would eventually wipe out most of her family. Her mother found work in a linen factory while her father returned to his trade, eager to redeem himself. Before long he slipped back into his old ways, with their single end regularly erupting in Saturday night violence. The small feisty girl would charge in to her mother's assistance with eyes ablaze and red hair flying, and be thrown out by her father, with the door barred against her until it was safe to let her in.

The morning after, while father Robert nursed his hangover, it was church as usual for the family, in neat Sunday clothes redeemed from the pawnshop the day before – a necessary procedure which constantly shamed their mother and caused embarrassment for Mary, the go-between. A patient and deeply religious woman, Mrs Slessor was determined to lead by example, and was especially concerned about her eldest daughter, for Mary was becoming known as a 'wild lassie'. Her mother emerged with her faith stronger than ever after the death of her eldest son, on whom she had pinned such hopes. However, his death, and the subsequent loss of two other children, may have played a significant part in her husband's downfall.

At 14 years old Mary, still small but more impetuous than ever, was a skilled weaver, working ten hours a day yet making time to go to night school. With the arrival of a seventh child and her father now doing only occasional labouring work, her wages were needed more than ever. Within a few years she was given two 60-inch power looms to operate, and permission to keep a textbook beside her, for she was determined to fill the gaps in her education, spurred on by the example of missionary and explorer David Livingstone (1813–73), who was largely self-educated. Her dry wit and lively sense of fun made her popular with her workmates, despite a growing tendency to try to convert them to her way of thinking.

With the death of her husband, Mrs Slessor's financial position improved and her burden of shame was lifted, for she no longer had to present a false image of respectability. Her remaining son John became apprenticed to a blacksmith and Mary's younger sister Susan began work as a 'half-timer', allowing them to move into slightly better accommodation, although still in a slum area.

By this time Mrs Slessor's carefully sown seeds had borne fruit, for Mary was now a fully committed Christian. An old neighbour had helped to prepare the ground earlier when she had taken the wild lassie in hand and put the fear of God into her, with dark threats of eternal damnation if she refused to mend her ways. Mary may have learned her lesson, but she never in the future resorted to such methods herself.

Her family attended the Wishart Memorial Church, which stood in the midst of slums at the east end of the Cowgate. W P Livingstone tells us:

Pends, or arched passages, led from the Cowgate into tall tenements with outside spiral stairs which opened upon a maze of landings and homes. Out of these sunless rookeries tides of young life poured by night and day, and spread over the neighbouring streets in undisciplined freedom.

Mary, already deeply involved in her church, had no hesitation in volunteering her services when a progressive new minister, James Logie, started up a mission nearby in Queen Street, near Quarry Pend – then an area with a particularly unsavoury reputation. Despite the veneer of toughness developed through her own chequered upbringing, she was shocked by the degree of human misery uncovered when she made a round of visits. Even so, this down-to-earth factory girl with an accent not unlike the locals' own was a welcome change to the usual run of 'do-gooders'. But it was the 'tides of young life' who concerned Mary most and here she found an unusual ally in James Logie, who set up the Victorian equivalent of a youth club, appreciating that the youngsters needed healthy recreation as well as spiritual nourishment, and an escape from the filthy streets and warrens where they played. So, with his blessing, she frequently took off to the countryside with a motley assortment of ragamuffins and gave them the time of their lives. Luckily Logie was spared the sight of his admirable young worker transformed into a bare-foot hoyden, skirts well above her knees, running races and climbing trees with the best of them.

Mary first proved her mettle one evening as she approached an empty shop used for Gospel meetings. Mission workers were supposed to travel around in pairs, a sensible precaution as they were considered fair game for abuse. However, Mary disregarded rules all her life and consequently was alone when a gang of youths surrounded her. When their ringleader began swinging a large chunk of lead attached to a string, around his head and outwards in her direction, she stared him out defiantly. He warned her to clear off and stop bothering them, perhaps an indication that she had already tried to persuade them into one of her meetings. She stood her ground but removed her Sunday hat in case it got damaged, and though he swung the lead nearer and nearer until it lightly grazed her forehead, she refused to give way. Then suddenly the lad capitulated and flung aside his weapon. 'She's game, boys,' he yelled, and with an about-turn, he pushed his reluctant pals into the meeting. Unforgettable words – they are recorded for posterity in Dundee's McManus Galleries in a stained glass window dedicated to Mary's memory. The same lads became regular helpers on her weekly expeditions to the country, but always with the warning, 'Mind, no strings'. Years later, on the wall of a mud hut in Africa, Mary would proudly display a photograph of the ring-leader with his wife and family, sent to her in grateful remembrance of a turning point in his life.

Mary's mission commitments left little time for outside interests or relationships. Possibly she scared off the local lads by appearing 'unco holy' – although she was never that – or perhaps she herself was scared off by the careless abandon of courting couples in closes and alleyways, and painful recollections of drunken couplings, unseen but unmistakable, within her own home. In a single end there were few secrets.

Her whole family monitored the progress of the missionaries abroad with intense interest, never missing opportunities to be present when a missionary on furlough regaled audiences with hair-raising accounts of adventures in faraway lands. For some it was pure enter-tainment, the equivalent of a night out at the cinema today, but not for the Slessors, who looked to the future when John, the second boy, might take the place of his brother Robert in the mission field. But this was not to be, for John also died prematurely. Mary's desire to become a woman missionary took root from this point and it was nurtured by the example of David Livingstone, who had once been a weaver himself.

Mary questioned her suitability for such work, for most of the missionaries, coming from professional backgrounds, were more confident and better educated. So she waited, and prayed for guidance. Seeking to make up lost ground, she broadened her reading, tackling Thomas Carlyle and John Milton, among other authors to whom she had been directed. She read as she walked to and from work, during work and long after it when she should have been asleep. But it was only when news of Livingstone's death in 1873 filtered through the following year, that her way became clear at last. She seized on one piece of his writing with wonder – published alongside his obituary, it seemed addressed to her alone: 'I direct your attention to Africa .... Do you carry on the work I have begun. I leave it with you.'

She applied to the Foreign Mission Board of the United Presbyterian Church for service in Calabar, one of the most godforsaken places on earth – or it had been until the first missionaries arrived 30 years before. It was said that no one travelling there bought a return ticket, for this was the area around the coast of West Africa known as the 'White Man's Grave'. Mary was entirely aware of this fact from the death notices which appeared with alarming regularity in the *Missionary Record*, the Church's magazine.

Mrs Slessor greeted the news with pride and delight, banishing fear from her mind; but her other daughters, Susan and young Janie, were less stoic, for Mary, sometimes bossy but always kindly and full of fun, had been the linchpin of the family. 'Why Calabar of all places?' they wanted to know. Mary said that she must go where she was most needed. With both of her sisters working by this time, she felt free to leave with a clear conscience.

Mary's application was accepted, backed up by a glowing reference from James Logie and further strengthened by a successful interview, with the proviso that during the interim period she should improve her English and extend her Bible knowledge. She was aware that she should also smooth out her accent, a mixture of broad Dundonian with lingering traces of her Aberdeen birthplace. Possessing minimal social graces, she was introduced to drawing-room manners for the first time by James Logie's wife, who was determined Mary should hold her head high among the resident Calabar missionaries. Mary privately considered this a waste of time, with so few drawing rooms in Calabar.

Finally Mary was sent to Moray House in Edinburgh for a three-month course of preparation. Later she said that some more practical training would have been more to the point. Then on 5 August 1876, at the age of 28, Mary set sail on the SS *Ethiopia* for West Africa, and when she finally arrived at her destination – Duke Town, the headquarters of the Calabar Mission – dressed in sober attire and regulation sun helmet, she looked every inch a Victorian lady missionary.

Chapter 2
First Impressions of Calabar

THE five weeks on the ship to Calabar were an extraordinary experience for Mary, who had never travelled beyond Edinburgh or Aberdeen. Although she was afraid of the sea, constant sunshine and warmth had begun to work their magic upon her, allaying her fears and easing the pain of parting from her family. Then, abruptly, her confidence was shattered when a storm blew up in the Bay of Biscay. Coming across her cowering on deck, a young ship's officer, whether prompted by genuine concern or merely wanting to strike up an acquaintance, was foolish enough to ask if she was frightened. Her terror vanished at once and, fired by indignation at being caught out, she answered with a flash of her usual spirit: 'God wouldnae send me all this way just to drown in your silly old ship.'

Some time after passing the Canary Islands and the headland of Cape Verde, the heat of the Dark Continent hit her and she experienced for the first time the seductive, indescribable smell of this part of Africa. The ship skirted the Ivory Coast and then the Gold Coast, bordered by mangrove forests stretching the entire length of the Guinea Coast. At various ports of call there was a brief opportunity to go ashore, which only increased Mary's impatience to reach her destination. The ship sailed on, passing the Mouths of the Niger and finally reaching the wide estuary of two rivers, the Cross and the Calabar, where the latter followed the Cross River's course inland on the last part of the journey.

Mary would have seen for herself the small islands where young lives had been sacrificed to placate the river gods, and the remains of the barracoons – grim reminders of the hundreds of thousands of slaves who were once penned there like cattle, to await their fate. The slave traders had wanted only the fittest and best and could afford to be selective; the remainder were expendable and many thousands of people were slaughtered. (The British Navy succeeded in blockading slave ships along the whole Guinea Coast and by 1840 this practice had ceased.)

About 50 miles from the sea, the *Ethiopia* turned east into the Calabar River which led to the anchorage of Old Calabar, dropping anchor off Duke Town. Mary's eyes were drawn instantly to the brightly painted wooden houses of chiefs and rich traders that were scattered around the hillside, amid an abundance of tropical greenery and rows of tall cottonwood trees. It made a charming picture and she was captivated by it. Yet she knew the early missionaries had lived there on a knife-edge, and malaria, against which there was still no protection, had decimated their numbers. James Luke, who arrived after Mary, wrote: 'For years as each new worker arrived, he was absorbed at the base, sent home or fell; and the days were marked by new graves in old ground.'

The areas of infested swampland escaped Mary's notice as with mounting excitement she identified Mission Hill, its cluster of white buildings, including the church and school, standing high above the town. The river was alive with colour and movement as paddlers in bright head-coverings and loincloths navigated their canoes between the hulks of old sailing ships which were roofed over and upgraded to provide storage and accommodation for traders. Palm oil, now a valuable commodity, had replaced human cargo as Calabar's principal export, and the oil traders' boats, piled high with containers, were competing in their race for Mary's ship. Identifying the red-capped Krumen (Liberian boatmen employed by the mission) who singled out the mission boat, Mary grabbed her bags, hoisted up her skirts and clattered down the stairs and along the decks in an unladylike dash for the point of disembarkation.

By the time she reached the shore she had regained some semblance of the dignity expected of a lady missionary – or more accurately a female agent, to give her correct designation. (She would wait several years to become a missionary in her own right.) A member of staff, Alexander Ross, had come out on the mission boat to meet her, and at the mission jetty was Mrs Sutherland, a veteran of many years and one of the few white women the Efik tribes honoured with the title of 'Akamba Ma' (Great Mother). With her were the schoolchildren, lined up and waiting in neat Sunday clothes to meet the latest arrival from Scotland. Beaming a welcome, they disarmed Mary completely, dispelling the shyness which could overwhelm her at unexpected moments. She gave a huge grin in response and, in convoy, they all climbed the steep hill to Mission House, where flowers bloomed in orderly profusion beside wild mango and banana trees.

Thirty years before, after land was allocated to the Calabar Mission, the missionaries discovered it was the official depository for dead slaves only when the ground was cleared for building and scores of corpses, in various stages of decomposition, were uncovered. When they also found it was a favourite hunting ground for leopards attracted by the prospect of an easy meal, King Eyamba was reminded that they were there at his invitation and he had promised protection. The king, mindful of the benefits his town was beginning to enjoy, consulted Egbo (or Ekpe) – a secret society controlling the entire region through a combination of terrorism and rough justice – who ordered the dumping ground to be sited elsewhere. A Nigerian, Professor Onwuka Dike, tells us: 'For all practical purposes the Egbo order was the supreme political power in Old Calabar; it exercised not only executive and legislative functions but was the highest court of appeal in the land.' The society came into existence in the absence of a hereditary ruler, for Eyamba and Eyo Honesty, albeit rich and influential chiefs, were kings in name only, despite ruling supreme over all except Egbo. While the rich could buy protection, when Egbo runners – grotesque in masks and bizarre costumes – whooped into town, stripping and scourging every woman and slave in their path, the place was cleared in an instant. Yet in times of disputes between the various Houses to which the entire community belonged, Egbo was beneficial in restoring law and order.

King Eyamba, although happy about 'Book' (education), had misgivings about the white God, but reached the conclusion that one more god was neither here nor there. On the other hand, King Eyo of Creek Town, given the name 'Honesty' by the traders for obvious reasons, would come to accept Christianity unconditionally. Both chiefs had become concerned about the amount of bloodletting in the area and supported the missionaries in their drive to eliminate acts of savagery, provided it didn't compromise their lifestyle.

The first area of conflict concerned the treatment of slaves. A privileged few were born into an influential House, were allocated land and eventually became as rich as any freeman, but the vast majority had a tenuous hold on life. When an important chief or his near relative died, slaves in their hundreds might be sacrificed to accompany him into the spirit world, a macabre funeral rite the pioneer missionaries fought long and hard to expurge. In 1849, on the death of King Eyamba, they watched in horror as his 30 wives and concubines, dressed in their finest attire, and mercifully drunk, were lowered into a huge pit in the floor of his 'Iron Palace', where, along with over 50 slaves, they were ritually murdered and buried beside him, his regalia, and food for the journey into the next world. The sole consolation was knowing the rest of Eyamba's slaves had escaped death temporarily by fleeing into the bush. The missionaries redoubled their efforts and the following year the 'Society for the Suppression of Human Sacrifices in Calabar' was formed, which included ten captains and three ships' surgeons. Pressure was applied to Eyamba's successor and Eyo of Creek Town, who promised that in future only criminals would be put to death – their compliance owing much to their desire to maintain a British influence in light of a possible takeover by the French. The Egbo Order also agreed to abide by this ruling; however, outwith the sphere of missionary influence, the practices continued.

Yet there were happier moments. Hope Waddell wrote: 'The dry season is playtime in Calabar … both farm labour and oil trading are suspended …. The evenings are spent by the young people in plays and games in the open.' He mentioned his own magic lantern shows which were attended by 'uproarious audiences', and the Africans in return performed miming plays, at which they excelled, for the missionaries. The good relations were confirmed by the large church attendances still being maintained when Mary Slessor arrived. Yet there were few communicants, for the Efiks were reluctant to forswear the age-old customs of polygamy and slave ownership in favour of church membership.

When Mary arrived at Mission House, the staff was out in force to welcome her. At this time the Scottish contingent consisted of four ordained missionaries, their wives and eight teachers, with an additional 18 African agents and one ordained African. The Mission's leader, the Rev. William Anderson, and his wife were on furlough when Mary arrived, but with practised ease – for she had done this many times – Mrs Sutherland drew the newcomer into the fold, also introducing her to Mammy Fuller, a West Indian ex-slave who had become an indispensable part of the Calabar Mission.

In Jamaica many years before, Hope Waddell had known many former slaves, still working in the sugar plantations, who originated from the Calabar region and talked nostalgically of their homeland. This prompted his desire to set up a mission there. The objective was twofold – to bring the Gospel to an area which had become degraded through the slave trade, and to repatriate Christian ex-slaves wishing to return, who would be valuable assets in the new field of mission. After its establishment, others followed from Jamaica – and Mammy Fuller was one of them. Mary felt at home with her immediately, but was wary of some of the others. However, her mentor, Mrs Sutherland, had been a bonnie fighter in the turbulent early days of the mission, and applied her Christianity in a down-to-earth manner, earning Mary's approval on both counts. Soon her mother was able to read in the *Missionary Record* that Miss Slessor had 'entered with strong hope and courage … and was a promising daughter to Mrs Sutherland'.

Mary's duties included teaching young children (mostly boys) in school, and in Sunday school, where the gender balance levelled out.

She also worked in the dispensary and visited the extended families of each House, whose living quarters were mud huts of varying size and importance within interconnecting yards. Professor Dike tells us that these Houses, which vied with each other for supremacy, were the direct result of the trade with the Europeans:

> *The mixture of peoples often meant that African law and culture vanished and a new law and order was evolved …. In its full development the House became at once a co-operative trading unit and a local government institution.*

At the entrance to each property stood a permanent armed guard and within the main yard was an ancestral shrine, complete with sacrificial offering. Although the head of each House might own hundreds of slaves, and a wealthy one up to a thousand, paradoxically the slaves often had more freedom than the so-called freewomen who were confined within the gates of the compound. This rule also applied to wives, unless supervising work on their farms under an armed guard. Over all of them their master held the power of life or death.

Mary enjoyed working with the children, and happily measured out medicines and treated bodies covered in sores with great care. (She was appalled by the amount of sores on every child's body and wrote home about their condition frequently at first.) However, visiting the compounds was an eye-opener. She was astonished by the Calabar practice of separating adolescent girls into 'fattening houses' where they were fed on the richest of food to prepare them for the marriage market, their prospective husbands believing that fat was beautiful as far as choosing a wife was concerned. Also surprising was the attitude of some of the more prosperous and allegedly Christian wives, whose smug piety and sense of superiority annoyed her intensely, making her escape to the slaves' quarters with a sense of relief. There she felt curiously at home as she learned to communicate with the women who, unlike the freewomen, had no pidgin English.

She was determined to master the language quickly, and had the help of an expert, the Rev. Hugh Goldie, formerly a missionary in

Jamaica but now in Creek Town a few miles away. (His Efik dictionary and Bible were to become standard works.) Having access to his books, she studied them intensely, fascinated by the intricate beliefs and customs of the Efik tribes. She discovered that the language came easily to her and was told by the natives that she was blessed with an Efik mouth – praise indeed for a wee Scots lassie.

Soon there was an opportunity to visit mission stations upriver where the way of life was simpler, and her idea of working in the interior probably was born at this time. She could tolerate the climate, apart from the harmattan ('the smokes') – the dry dusty wind blowing in from the Sahara each December which invaded the eyes, ears and throats of everyone – and she had seen filth before in the overcrowded slums of her childhood. But already she felt her time was wasted in a place well served by missionaries, with so great a need elsewhere. She also found the form of hierarchy (established by the trade in slaves whom it continued to exploit) within this affluent community hard to accept, as to a lesser degree was the exacting formality demanded after the Andersons returned from furlough.

They made a formidable pair: 'Daddy' Anderson who would battle with anyone on behalf of the Efiks; and his wife who ran Mission House 'with a rod of iron', but mothered a houseful of abandoned children. She and the new female agent clashed right from the outset, for Mary, ever careless of time, often overslept when given the responsibility of arousing the household. Once, in an effort to redeem herself, she wakened the whole household in the middle of the night, mistaking moonlight for the dawn. When she began turning up late at mealtimes, Mrs Anderson decided enough was enough and announced that in future Miss Slessor would go hungry if she persisted in her ways – which she did on several occasions.

Sundays were a particular trial, when Mission House offered hospitality after the English service to Europeans who happened to be in port, and Mary blessed Mrs Logie in Dundee for having the foresight to drum a few social niceties into her. In a letter to a friend of factory days, David Stewart, she wrote:

*I am now, as you know, among quite a different class of people from that I
was accustomed to at home. The European Society apart from the members of
the Mission are merchants, the government officials, the commanders, doctors and
pursers of the Steamers, Travellers … etc. etc. But though I value the refinement,
education, etc. of such society, I hope to be in fair with the dear old friends at
home.*

When the Mission House regime overwhelmed her, Mary would slip
away to the bush, out of sight, and fling off the trappings which were
the bane of her life – the regulation sun hat, thick stockings and boots.
Barefoot much of her childhood, she would now wiggle her toes in
delight before racing along the path to climb any tree of her fancy,
petticoats discarded in a heap on the ground. It worked every time.
Later she confessed to having climbed every tree worthy of the name in
the area, an indication that the wild lassie was still alive and beginning
to kick.

The mission was an ever open door for unwanted infants and Mary
developed a great fondness for them. Twins rescued by the missionaries
seemed especially precious, and nothing provoked her to such fury as
their wanton murder. Their persecution and that of their mothers
arose from an inherent belief that a devil had fathered one of the
children and, without knowing which, both had to be destroyed.
Eventually, in 1878, when a treaty was implemented between the
Calabar chiefs and Consul Hopkins, the British representative
stationed on the island of Fernando Po (Bioko) in the Bight of Biafra,
Mary, like everyone who had worked towards this goal, was overjoyed.
Human sacrifice and twin murders were now punishable by death, as
was administration of the poison bean ordeal, where guilt or innocence
was determined by making the accused swallow a potion containing
the deadly Calabar *esere* bean. If he or she vomited up the mixture,
which was unlikely, it proved their innocence. The treaty also stated
that the mourning period for widows – previously segregated for years
in a state of filth and near starvation – would be only one month, while
the 'abominable, disgraceful and barbarous custom' of Egbo runners

stripping and indecently assaulting any woman wearing a dress or covering was 'forever abolished'. Mary described the moment she first heard the news in a letter to Sunday school children in Dundee:

Just as it became dark one evening I was sitting in my verandah talking to the children, when we heard the beating of drums and the singing of men coming near. This was strange, because we are on a piece of ground which no one in the town has a right to enter. Taking the wee twin boys in my hands I rushed out, and what do you think I saw? A crowd of men standing outside the fence chanting and swaying their bodies. They were proclaiming that all twins and twin- mothers could now live in the town, and if anyone murdered the twins or harmed the mothers he would be hanged by the neck. If you could have heard the twin-mothers who were there, how they laughed and clapped their hands and shouted 'Sosono! Sosono!' (Thank you! Thank you!) you will not wonder that amidst all that noise I turned aside and wept tears of joy and thankfulness, for it was a glorious day for Calabar.

Despite her joy over this monumental breakthrough, Mary's thoughts inevitably turned to places untouched by the new order. She began to badger William Anderson about working inland, but always received the same reply – it was no place for a woman on her own. A seed of doubt began to grow as she wondered if she had misinterpreted God's plan for her, all this time becoming increasingly debilitated through recurring bouts of malaria. Early in 1879, after a particularly severe attack (to paraphrase her own words), she looked as if she had escaped from a lunatic asylum.

During this last illness she revised her opinion of 'Mammy' Anderson, whose touch was gentle when Mary needed it most; but she was left with an overwhelming longing for home. The normal tour of duty for missionaries at this time was four years – later extended to five, followed by a year off – but the Andersons looked again at Mary, so uncharacteristically subdued, recognised her need, and sent her home a year early. As they waved her goodbye they may have wondered if she would ever return.

Chapter 3
A Real Missionary at last

AT first Mary was content just to be reunited with her family, but as her energy returned other factors took over. Her first priority was to prevail on them to move to a healthier area; the thin white face of Janie, her 'delicate' younger sister, had been enough to convince her of this. As usual, when Mary made up her mind action quickly followed, and before they had time to reconsider, her mother and sisters were settled into a house in Dowansfield, on the outskirts of Dundee. Although it meant earmarking more of her salary of £60 a year to send home, she considered it a small price to pay.

However, to her surprise, Mary found that she was becoming as homesick for the bright clear skies of Africa as she had been earlier for the dark tenements of home. Even in her home church, the contrast was marked. In Duke Town the Efiks, whether converted or not, praised the Lord with joyful abandon, but here church praise was a solemn affair. Despite the congregation's attempts to 'Sing to the Lord with cheerful voice', it was clear that the Africans could give them lessons in cheerfulness.

By now fighting fit, she took James Logie's advice and approached the Foreign Mission Board in Edinburgh requesting a transfer to anywhere in Calabar District other than Duke Town, although she conceded she would return there if necessary. Her leave was extended by four months, during which time she was expected to travel around the countryside speaking at meetings of her experiences in Calabar, in order to raise funds and encourage recruitment.

Mary was full of contradictions. In Africa she was able to confront hostile tribesmen fearlessly, but back home she was afraid to enter a field of cows, or to cross an Edinburgh street. In this instance her fear was centred around addressing middle-class congregations. Deeply conscious of her lack of formal education, the sight of men in an audience particularly upset her, this response perhaps triggered by memories of her father whose behaviour had made her wary of men in general. However, speaking at informal meetings to women from her own background she had no problems; nor with children towards whom she could relate easily. At such times her natural spontaneity took over and she could hold her listeners enthralled. So deep an impression did she make on two Falkirk schoolgirls, Janet Wright and Martha Peacock, that they would later volunteer for service in Calabar and become invaluable to her at critical stages of her life.

She was now impatient to go back to Africa, and on discovering the Creek Town missionary Hugh Goldie – also on furlough – was about to return, she arbitrarily decided to accompany him, pre-empting the Mission Board's arrangements. The opportunity to glean more information on the Efiks during the voyage was too good to miss, for there was none more knowledgeable than Hugh Goldie.

Back in Calabar, to her joy she was assigned to an outstation at Old Town, two miles upriver from Duke Town, where she would be alone, apart from a young Efik woman and several older children detailed to assist her. Still under the surveillance of William Anderson, Mary was determined to prove herself fit for the pioneer work on which her mind was set. Old Town was one of four places where the missionaries had begun work in 1846. Its chief, Willie Tom Robbins, despite adopting a British name, had remained impervious to all attempts at reform. On his deathbed nine years later, overruling the combined efforts of the British consul, missionaries and sea captains, plus the full weight of the reformed Egbo law, he ordered his wives, sons, freemen and slaves to be seized as hostages to await his death, after which they were slaughtered. The resulting outcry from the Europeans forced the British consul to take the kind of action the missionaries deplored. After giving prior warning, HMS *Antelope* sailed in, carefully trained its sights on the town and blasted it out of existence – a customary way of dealing with such problems at this time.

Since then, although rebuilt, it had never fully recovered, despite efforts by mission staff, especially Mrs Sutherland, on its behalf.

The mission house, built of mud and palm thatch, had been vacant for some time and was in a bad state of repair. However, Mary was impatient to move in and worked alongside the Krumen sent from Duke Town to make it habitable. These particular Africans, originating from Liberia, were noted for their seamanship, and many found work at the port of Old Calabar. Others, employed as boatmen to the mission, also did general work for it, for they were reliable and loyal to their employers. As a reluctant passenger, Mary had often been transported upriver by the Krumen, who recognised her fear of water and helped her to overcome it. She welcomed them to Old Town as old friends.

Already Mary was asserting her new independence – the wretched sun helmet had gone and, except on Sundays, she took to working in a plain cotton dress, her bare feet encased in plimsolls. With several thousand people contained within twenty square miles of bush, she discovered she had her work cut out. But at last she had the chance to be a real missionary and she plunged headlong into the challenge, with the local people, reassured by her lack of pretension, quick to respond. Before long she had established small outstations in Qua and other neighbouring villages and her days were filled with teaching, preaching, administering first aid and dispensing medicine. Outwith Old Town which had its own church/school, she held services where she could – in palaver houses (similar to village halls), under a tree or in a chief's compound, and grew accustomed to one high-ranking chief taking his place beside the children each school day.

Leaving her young Efik assistant in charge, Mary began to travel further afield, accompanied by two boys from the mission, sometimes spending the night in a village, sleeping native style on a bench in a mud hut. Having almost conquered her fear of water, it was replaced by another terror – the bush by night, when the forests came to life, and unseen creatures screeched and snarled in the darkness. Had her Efik boys not been equally afraid of incurring their Ma's wrath, they would have taken off in a cloud of dust. Mary said later that she had never properly appreciated the story of Daniel and the lions until she heard leopards growling in the bush. 'Oh God of Daniel, shut their mouths!' she would pray often as she forced herself forward.

In his book *Mary Slessor of Calabar*, published in 1915, the year of her death, W P Livingstone tells us:

> *The people found her different from other missionaries, she would enter their townships as one of themselves ... and get right into their confidence ... so many diseased and maimed crowded to her that she would miss the tide twice over.*

With no medical training, she found the experience gained in Duke Town invaluable when dealing with everyday ailments, but had only quinine or painkillers to deal with more serious problems. The advice of Hope Waddell to patients 30 years before still held good: 'Use no native medicine, employ no native doctor, drink no rum, pray to Jesus for a blessing, and praise him for recovery.' Soon, however, Mary learned that some of the native remedies were not to be scorned and she became adept at recognising the healing properties of certain indigenous plants.

Two deputies from the Foreign Mission Board in Edinburgh, Messrs Marshall and Williamson, came to inspect the work of the mission during 1881/82. After paying Mary a visit, they reported that she was a devoted and energetic agent and sustained her manifold duties cheerfully. They also said they were worn out by the end of it. On a Sunday, with Mary acting as interpreter, one of them conducted a service in a palaver house with a clay floor, round which the skulls of old enemies were imbedded. One skull had worked loose and somehow ended up between the deputy's feet, to his considerable surprise, a fact also mentioned in the report. There was a special recommendation that Miss Slessor be permitted to continue working alone in Old Town 'because she prefers this manner of life to being associated with another white person on a station'.

It had been a difficult year for the mission. William Anderson had suffered a collapse. Then both Mrs Sutherland and Mrs Anderson became terminally ill – two indomitable women whose deaths were mourned by Africans and Europeans alike. Consequently, the timing was wrong when Alexander Ross – the missionary who first welcomed Mary to Calabar – began objecting to Anderson's tolerant attitude towards the unconverted, which sparked off such a furore that Ross was forced to resign. He then set up an alternative church nearby, which splintered the mission and confused the Efiks, who wondered if there were now two white Gods in Duke Town. It seems likely that such a disruption triggered the visit from the deputies, the first since the mission's inception. They were certainly caught up in it, and although their report side-tracked the outcome, it appears that the life of the rival church was brief. Sadly, one of the deputies, Mr Williamson, contracted fever and was buried at sea three days into the return voyage.

Some believed that Mary had chosen this solitary life for economic reasons, for at Duke Town the cost of imported food made boarding expensive, whereas in Old Town she could live cheaply on native produce, which enabled her to send home most of her salary. They found it impossible to accept that she would live this way from choice. Nevertheless, for one of Mary's temperament it was perhaps the only way.

She became almost fanatical in her defence of twins, for the treaty drawn up a few years before, outlawing their murder, had only been partially effective in the neighbourhood of Old Town. Immediately there was news of a twin birth, she dropped everything and raced to the rescue, and the mission house was soon full of twin babies and other unwanted children. Although she became devoted to them, they hampered her work despite help from her young assistant and the older house children. This prompted her suggestion to the Mission Board that an orphanage might be set up in Duke Town with a missionary in charge, and staffed by local girls. 'If such a crowd of twins should come to her as I have to manage she would require to devote all her time to them.' Like many of her ideas it wasn't followed up, and she was seldom without a child in her arms or in her bed at night. By then their small feet were firmly in the door.

This was one of the differences between Mary Slessor and other missionaries. Every mission house had its share of unwanted children, who were looked after in a separate part of the house by Efik women – but with Mary there was a personal involvement from the start. Early on she had been counselled to maintain a level of detachment and remember she was a missionary, not an African – advice which she scorned, for it ran counter to her belief that all were equal in the sight of God.

One particular aspect of life in Calabar which outraged her sense of justice was trading, over which the Efik middlemen held the monopoly, with upriver tribes likely to lose their lives if they attempted to break it. As a result they had no outlet for their marketable goods. Therefore Mary felt no compunction in encouraging them to circumvent Efiks who were picketing a trading factory adjacent to the mission, and led them, under cover of darkness, through inviolate mission land which allowed quick access to the factory. While fellow missionaries may have questioned this use of her privileged position, she won the respect of the traders and the gratitude of upriver farmers, who in a surge of renewed confidence responded in great numbers, eventually forcing the middlemen to release their stranglehold.

On one of her travels Mary met Okon, a chief from Ibaka (later known as James Town), situated on the Cross estuary about 30 miles distant. She made such an impression that Okon was determined she should pay his people a visit, offering his own canoe for the journey. Discussing the matter with King Eyo VII, who was a Christian and had become a personal friend, Eyo insisted that Mary must travel in style in one of his royal canoes, a grand affair 40 feet long, which employed 33 paddlers of great expertise. He told her she must arrive 'not as a stranger to a strange people, but as a lady and our mother'.

Predictably, on the day of departure the royal canoe arrived many hours late, but was freshly painted in Mary's honour. More delay followed *en route* to the riverside, for she had to embrace every free-woman enclosed in her compound and every child lining the way. Bombarded on all sides by advice from well-wishers who uttered dire threats should she be harmed, Mary found the whole community had turned out for the occasion. Comfortable places were found in the canoe for the four house children she insisted on taking, and more farewells had to be said before she settled amidships among ricebags intended as a present. Darkness fell, torches were lit, but nobody except perhaps Mary seemed in a hurry to break the carnival mood. Then finally the drummers who kept time for the paddlers were in place, 33 paddles were dipped, and the canoe glided away into the darkness.

The crewmen's adeptness dispersed the remnant of Mary's fear, and she relaxed, lulled by their deep voices softly singing improvised nonsense in time to their paddling. At one point she was the subject of their song, to her considerable amusement and the hilarity of the children: 'Our beautiful Ma is with us Ho Ho Ho,' they sang repeatedly, the pauses occurring as the paddles were dipped. Many hours later the canoe touched land and she was carried, despite protestations, over the beach and ceremoniously deposited in Okon's compound beside an assortment of farm animals.

As an honoured guest she was given Okon's own hut, which led into the quarters of the women, who found her an ongoing source of curiosity. Never having seen a white woman before – especially one with red hair and deep blue eyes – they touched her, examined her clothing and observed her every movement, forcing Mary to hang a sheet at the entrance at times for privacy. The nights were the worst, for the chief wives, to prevent her feeling lonely, slept with her, packed side by side like king-size sardines in a tin. With their perspiration flowing freely in the heat of Okon's hut, this was a kindly native custom Mary could have done without.

She did her utmost to fulfil Okon's expectations, teaching the native children simple spelling and arithmetic and tending their sores, as well as treating various other ailments. Nevertheless her main purpose was to impart the basic tenets of Christianity, no mean undertaking in the space of two weeks. She lay down each night exhausted, and soon neither perspiring wives, lizards nor even rats were able to keep her awake.

During Mary's visit a tornado tore the roof off the chief's hut, and although Mary managed to sweep the children from danger, she succumbed to fever after being drenched to the skin. On her recovery, she faced her first serious encounter.

Two 16 year-old girls had escaped from their elderly master's compound to visit young men who offered a welcome diversion. Having broken a fundamental moral code, both girls were sentenced to a hundred lashes, from which they were unlikely to recover. On hearing this, Mary angrily confronted Okon, who warned her the elders would say that 'God's word be no good if it destroy the power of the law to punish evildoers'. But he eventually agreed, in deference to his guest, to reconvene the court and allow her to speak on the girls' behalf.

When all were present Mary first addressed the offending girls:

You have brought much shame on us by your folly and by abusing your master's confidence .... Though God's Word teaches us to be merciful, it does not countenance or pass over sin, and I cannot shelter you from punishment. You have knowingly and deliberately brought it upon yourselves. Ask God to keep you in the future so that your conduct may not be a reproach to yourselves and the word of God which you know.

The elders were smug in this vindication of their judgment, until she swung round suddenly and wiped the smiles from their faces:

Ay, but you are really to blame. It is your system of polygamy which is a disgrace to you and a cruel injustice to these helpless women. Sixteen-year-old girls are not beyond the age of fun and frolic. To confine them as you do is a shame and a blot on your manhood: obedience such as you command is not worth the having.

Uproar followed and Mary wondered if she had gone too far. However Okon silenced the gathering, reminding them she was their guest and they had much cause to be grateful to her, and after prolonged discussion, the punishment was reduced to ten strokes. She thanked the court for its clemency and asked the girls to show their gratitude by willing and faithful service. Afterwards she tried to block out their screams as thick alligator hide bit cruelly into their bodies, running to their assistance the moment the punishment ceased.

Back in Okon's hut, Mary administered painkillers and gently tended their wounds, promising the girls protection until their recovery. She pondered over the tribe's future; it was unlikely that one woman alone could effect any permanent change within the space of a fortnight. Yet she believed she wasn't alone, which made all the difference.

Mary was travelling back in Okon's canoe, and to express their appreciation he and his principal wife decided to accompany her. Soon after setting out a violent storm erupted and the craft began to pitch wildly out of control, with the crew becoming paralysed with fright. This was Mary's nightmare scenario. However, with her children's safety paramount, she took a grip of herself and sharply ordered the paddlers to do the same. She directed them to head for the bank and grab overhanging branches, which succeeded in preventing the canoe from capsizing. The children, half-submerged and already terrified by the thunder and lightning, clung to her desperately, and only her presence as she sang softly to reassure them prevented them becoming hysterical. The storm subsided as quickly as it had arisen, but before long Mary began shuddering uncontrollably, and the chief and his wife held her close in an effort to transmit heat from their own bodies. When they arrived at Old Town she had a raging fever and had to be carried to the mission house. To her relief the children had come to no harm.

A further storm lifted the mission house roof off and Mary and her household had to shelter temporarily in the traders' quarters next door, before being forced to return to Duke Town. There her malaria returned with a vengeance and she was invalided home in April 1883.

Chapter 4
Tragic Prelude to the Okoyong

BEFORE her latest bout of malarial fever, Mary had rescued a pair of twins whom relatives were bent on destroying. When they succeeded in killing the boy, Mary had a constant vigil kept over his twin sister and at the point of departure refused to leave unless the baby went with her. William Anderson, equally intractable when the occasion demanded, was adamant that the child must be left behind for, apart from Mary being in no fit state to look after her, involvement to such a degree was directly opposed to missionary policy. The deadlock was only broken when Anderson realised her genuine distress, and in a moment of compassion relented, a decision he would have cause to rejoice over later.

Both Mary and the baby were carried aboard the ship, where there was no lack of volunteer carers, for the surviving twin, like most African infants, was a beautiful child. The weeks of sea air and rest hastened Mary's recovery, although she was still weak on her arrival at Dundee. Waiting to welcome her were her mother and sisters, and as she stepped forward to greet them with the black baby in her arms, she exploded with laughter at the astonishment on their faces.

She had the infant baptised in the Wishart Memorial Sunday School as Jean Annan Slessor after her sister Janie, confirming a relationship which would hold fast until Mary's death. After she fully recovered, she was expected to carry out the same round of lecture tours as before, but this time attention was focused on the baby whom she insisted on taking with her. The bright-eyed African child proved an instant success, a living and breathing example of a twin who had survived, therefore a hundred times more interesting than the usual kind of memorabilia the missionaries brought back.

At no time did Mary try to exploit the situation – she simply grew so fond of the child that she never considered going anywhere without her. Nevertheless wee Janie touched the hearts of everyone, and money poured in to support the work of the mission. As a result, in January 1884, when Mary reported to the Mission Board that she was well enough to return to Calabar, she was asked to postpone her departure and carry out another round of lecture tours. Finally in December, having fulfilled her obligations, she was on the point of sailing when the first of a series of disasters struck.

It had been obvious for some time that her sister Janie's health had further deteriorated. Her consumption, a condition so often clothed in euphemisms in the Victorian age, was never directly referred to by Mary's first biographer, W P Livingstone; but the facts spoke for themselves, and Mary's fears were confirmed when the family learned that Janie was unlikely to survive unless she moved to a warmer climate. At this point Mary's usual common sense deserted her. She convinced herself that Calabar could provide the warm climate required, completely losing sight of the area's reputation at that time as one of the unhealthiest places on earth. In a moment of desperation and madness she wrote to the Mission Board in Edinburgh, requesting permission to take her sister back with her. She frankly explained the reason but gave the assurance that they would segregate themselves, thus proving no threat to others.

Needless to say, Edinburgh vetoed the idea, but generously allowed Mary time to sort out her problems. While she cast about wildly for another solution, a friend suggested a move to the kindlier climate of Devon, where the Slessors were offered the use of a house in Topsham, near Exeter. This was enough to spur Mary into action and she whisked Janie off immediately, while their mother, whose own health was questionable, followed shortly afterwards. Her sister Susan chose to remain behind.

Both Janie and her mother seemed to be benefiting from the soft pure air and pleasant environment, and the family began to settle, making new friends within the local Congregational church. Then came the news that Susan had suddenly and inexplicably died in Edinburgh while visiting an old friend of Mary's, Mrs McCrindle. They were only beginning to recover from this blow when Mrs Slessor also became ill with tuberculosis. Mary recognised her loyalties now lay with her family and accordingly tendered her resignation to the Mission Board, which assured her that her place would be held open, should she ever wish to return.

Two year-old Janie provided a ray of brightness on an otherwise bleak landscape, giving Mary's mother and sister an incentive to recover, and gradually the health of both improved. In need of an income, Mary found part-time work in Exeter hospital, where the experience would prove useful if ever the way opened for her return to Calabar. She also began to take an active part in the work of the Congregational Church.

However, with Mrs Slessor's relative improvement came her determination that Mary should go back to West Africa. This time she was the one to dig in her heels. 'You are my child given to me by God, and I have given you back to him,' she had said in the beginning and reiterated now. Mary reassessed the situation, and after much prayerful consideration bowed to her mother's wishes and her own conviction that God wanted her to return.

Accordingly she set the procedure in motion and was scheduled to sail on 11 November 1885. Then suddenly the health of both her mother and Janie deteriorated once more. Mrs Slessor was adamant that Mary should sail as planned, and only with the help of an old friend in Dundee – who was prepared to look after the household in her absence – and the promised support of their new church friends, was it possible for her to leave.

Why she did so, when it was unlikely that she would see either of them again, is hard to understand. But Mary and her mother shared a faith so strong that they were prepared to sacrifice everything in the cause of the Gospel. Mrs Slessor's passionate belief that God had a purpose for Mary in Africa had become her principal reason for living and Mary knew to deny her this would almost certainly hasten her decline. She believed God had used her mother to open the door for her return, and the ultimate test of her faith was to walk through it. The financial aspect may have also played some part, for her assured salary as a missionary was needed to sustain the family, their other source of income having ceased with Susan's death. Mary's reasons for leaving may have been understandable – the timing was less so.

On her return to Calabar, Mary was assigned to Creek Town, for Hugh Goldie was now working at base. Disappointed at not being reunited with the people of Old Town and its environs, with whom she had built a strong bond, she nonetheless recognised King Eyo's presence in Creek Town would be of considerable help. Educated at the mission, King Eyo VII (Eyo Honesty's successor) was a practising Christian, temperate in an area renowned for its drunkenness, faithful to his one and only wife, and altogether an exemplary figure from the missionary point of view. Quite early on, Mary found his lively enquiring mind matched her own and an unlikely friendship developed between the former mill-girl from Dundee and the powerful African chief. Interested in learning more about Scotland, he had even written to her mother, a red-letter day indeed for Mrs Slessor whose stock rose accordingly when the word went around.

During her two and a half years' absence, conditions in Calabar had altered, with new mission recruits and a resident British Consul installed in Duke Town, following the establishment of the Oils Rivers Protectorate. This had come into existence after Germany had annexed the neighbouring Cameroons, when British Baptist missionaries were thrown out and their houses repossessed. Such a development had sent a frisson of alarm not only through the missionary fraternity in Calabar, but throughout the whole population.

However, for Mary perhaps the greatest achievement had been the arrival of the mission's own steam launch, bought by Sunday school children from all over Scotland, who had raised over a thousand pounds in farthings and ha'pennies to buy it. Coming in the wake of many months of intinerating by Mary – when she had visited Sunday schools all over the land – could this be coincidental?

The *Smoking Canoe*, as the Efiks called the launch, allowed quick access to the upriver stations of Ikonetu and Ikorofiong and beyond, where the younger missionaries had recently succeeded in breaking the Cross River blockade and obtaining the tribes' permission to install an African teacher in the townships of Umon and Ikotana. Yet when Consul Johnston attempted to go further than Umon, with the aim of establishing free trading, he reported being repelled by the tribe with 'a hail of slugs', then chased downriver by cannibals 'bent on eating' his Krumen.

If there had been any doubt over the rightness of Mary's decision to leave Britain when she did, she was paying the penalty now, for her days were stalked by anxiety and her nights haunted by it. In a fever of impatience she waited for news, and when it finally came early in January 1886 she was awash with relief to be told the health of both invalids had improved. In a letter already waiting to return with the steamer, she added a tremulous postscript:

> *I was hardly able to wait for your letters and then I rushed to my room and behaved like a silly body, as if it had been bad news. It brought you all so clearly before me. At Church I sat beside the King and cried quietly into my wrap all evening.*

Her mother never received her letter, for she had died three days before. At the news Mary became submerged in grief and self-recrimination, and when Janie died three months later her desolation was complete. With the last of her family gone, she wrote to a friend:

> *I, who all my life have been caring and planning and living for them, am left as it were, stranded and alone. There is no one to write and tell all my stories and nonsense to. Heaven is now nearer to me than Britain ....*

She had also written, 'No one will be anxious about me if I go up-country', an indication that despite the rawness of her grief her thoughts were already turning towards pioneer work.

Shortly afterwards she approached William Anderson with a bold plea regarding going upriver to the Okoyong, a largely unknown territory of dense forest land contained between the Cross and Calabar Rivers. The tribe was Bantu-speaking, although familiar with the Efik dialect, and was believed to have migrated westward at some point from Central Africa. W P Livingstone described the entire region as being enclosed with a fence of terrorism as impenetrable as a ring of steel, and reports of atrocities perpetrated by the Okoyong were legend.

Mary's desire to go there, born several years earlier, would have been rekindled anyhow, but now it was fuelled by her need to justify herself in the aftermath of her grief. She found the two senior missionaries, Anderson and Goldie, remarkably understanding at this time. Both had earlier recognised her potential for pioneer work which she would never fulfil shackled within the restraints of Calabar, yet Anderson was deeply reluctant to sanction this undertaking. Despite knowing he was wasting his breath, he highlighted the risks involved, reminding her that others had tried to go and narrowly escaped with their lives. When she refused to be moved, the Mission Committee agreed to consider her request and in July 1886 made formal application to the Board in Edinburgh, stressing that the Okoyong was the place of Miss Slessor's own choice.

Hugh Goldie had already familiarised Mary with the tribe's background:

> *The Okoyong rejoice in a wild freedom and this feeling, with their distrust of each other, separates them so that each family has its own settlement in the bush, living a life of thorough independence ... their dread of the power of spells is so great that they arm themselves when they go out and when they sit down to partake of food .... This cloud of dread overhangs the whole of their life ... leading them to occasional escape from it in wild drunken revelry .... All the customs which have been abandoned in Calabar still prevail amongst them.*

Soon Mary would raise a derisory eyebrow at Goldie's description of occasional bouts of 'drunken revelry', when it was commonplace for her to go to sleep knowing she was the only adult sober within miles.

King Eyo, whose subjects had successfully defeated the Okoyong in a bloody battle some years earlier, told her that Okoyong women were as fierce as their men and had dragged away their wounded to prevent heads being taken. Instead of dissuading her, this information filled Mary with admiration, although she was probably prudent enough to keep this to herself. A truce had been finally called because the Okoyong had no wish to cut off their only source of gin, gunpowder and chains, but they still considered themselves at war with the Efiks, for Eyo had refused to sanction their custom of burying a slave alive to ratify the peace.

During this time, accompanied by a small group of missionaries, Mary ventured three times into Okoyong territory to try to negotiate a deal. Allowed past the sentries at the tribal village of Ekenge only because they were unarmed and offered something for nothing, they were met each time with suspicion and surrounded by armed guards, although given a hearing and allowed to depart unharmed. By the end of the third visit, the tribe admitted their desire for the education the Efiks enjoyed, but their suspicions remained and no further progress was made. Mary reported that one or two of the chiefs seemed in favour of accepting her, but in a mastery of understatement admitted 'as a body they were not very enthusiastic'. However if they weren't impressed, Mary certainly was, commenting that physically they were a far higher type of man than the Calabar people. 'The nose is higher, the mouth and chin finer, the eyes fearless and piercing.'

She waited over 18 months while her case was debated in Edinburgh, and it was June 1888 before she knew the outcome was successful. Towards the cost of a mission house she had been granted the sum of £50. Immediately she set off for Ekenge alone to settle matters once and for all and again the royal canoe was put at her disposal. This time the paddlers were less enthusiastic, knowing their heads would be on poles if the Okoyong laid hands on them. The canoe was carpeted and provided with cushions and food for Mary's comfort, thoughtful tokens of Eyo's concern for her, which she deeply appreciated for her own courage was beginning to flag.

She was put ashore at the landing beach, then the canoe made off quickly to the other side of the river out of firing range. Four miles along a single track through dense forest lay Ekenge, where its sentries stepped back in surprise at the sight of a lone unarmed white woman and allowed her to pass. This time the reception was warmer, with the Okoyongs clearly impressed that she had arrived alone, surely a sign of courage and good intent. Chief Edem, as head of the Ekenge branch of Egbo, called a palaver to discuss the matter. Mary's forthright manner must have tipped the balance, for they decided in her favour and accepted her conditions: they would allocate her land which would be sacrosanct and she in return would teach them about her God and 'Book' and give them such medical care as she could.

Edem told her she was wasting her time going to Ifako, a village two miles distant, as the chiefs were having a celebration and would all be drunk, but he hospitably offered her a hut for the night. There she met his sister, Ma Eme, a woman of obvious character to whom she was drawn instantly. Mary insisted on safe conduct for the paddlers and added eight more miles to her day by bringing them back from the safe haven of the canoe – at least those brave enough to risk it, after learning they had been granted a special dispensation. They grouped around her and joined in the singing as she held a short service of thanksgiving, while the Okoyongs looked on with amazement. This isolated incident demonstrated the mutual trust she demanded from opposing factions, and that all agreed to abide by her rules pinpointed her first victory.

The following day the chiefs in Ifako were nursing a hangover but, intent in keeping up with their Ekenge neighbours, with whom, uncharacteristically, relations were good, they also allocated ground and agreed to her conditions. She walked on air the six miles back to the landing place, where Eyo's boys couldn't wait to shoot off down-river before their dispensation ran out.

Mary reported the outcome to the senior missionaries, and she arranged to leave Creek Town on 4 August 1888, with the kindly Eyo, despite his opposition to her going to the Okoyong, once more offering his royal canoe and paddlers for the journey. This time they would also have to transport Mary's current household of five orphans, including five year-old Janie, along with several bearers to carry their belongings on the final trek through the forest. The news had spread like wildfire throughout Calabar, and colleagues pleaded and villagers wept in an effort to dissuade her. Even a delegation of traders arrived from Duke Town to try to make her see sense. 'It's a gunboat they need, not a missionary,' they told her.

On the morning of departure the rain fell in torrents, and continued unabated as the bearers, their bodies glistening with water, made equally heavy weather of the loading. After a sleepless night Mary was hard pressed to keep her temper as precious hours were squandered, until King Eyo arrived to supervise the loading and give moral support. This she desperately needed, worn down by outpourings of grief and forecasts of impending disaster from the Efiks gathered to see her off. Her more inhibited colleagues were also concerned, and when Hugh Goldie watched her finally go aboard with the children, on impulse he called for a volunteer to escort her to her destination. William Bishop, the mission printer, responded without hesitation and took his place in the canoe beside Mary, earning a heartfelt smile of gratitude. Then the crew reached for their paddles and they were finally on their way.

Chapter 5
'It's a Gunboat they need, not a Missionary'

O N Mary's first forays into the Okoyong heartland, she had been struck by the beauty of her surroundings as the canoe glided smoothly upriver, casting mirror images in its path. Then the banks had been lush with greenery and exotic flowers, creating the illusory promise of an enchanted kingdom beyond. Now, in the rainy season, it was a very different landscape and the river was turbulent, causing her to grip Bishop's arm in alarm on several occasions. The paddlers had to struggle to make headway and by the time they reached the landing beach it was already dusk.

Mary decided to go on ahead and seek help from the tribe while Bishop supervised the unloading. By this time her priority was shelter for the children, although rain meant little to them compared with walking through a forest growing darker by the minute. A boy of eleven, in a show of bravado, led the unwilling procession carrying a box of food on his head, followed by another, eight years old and less stoic, with pots and a kettle. Five year-old Janie and a boy two years younger came next, both already weeping, while Mary brought up the rear carrying an infant and a bundle of clothes.

She chivvied them onwards with promises of home-made toffee and sang nonsense songs to block out the sounds of the forest and keep up their spirits. 'Our singing would discourage any self-respecting leopard,' she once wrote to a friend, but on this occasion she had to sing alone and pray that this was enough to scare predators away. For four miles they slithered their way through mud and forestation, each vague shape presenting a threat, each new sound striking terror in their hearts. Every African child knew the forests concealed beasts of prey and evil spirits, and Mary's orphans were no exception. Forced to the pace of the youngest, by the time they approached Ekenge even the eleven year-old was crying. Mary, sick at heart for the ordeal she had put them through, was close to tears herself.

She was puzzled by the absence of watchfires and guards surrounding the village, and that there was no sign of life within it. In the direction of Ifako, two miles away, came the only sounds to disturb the silence. There was either a battle or a celebration in progress – it was often hard to tell the difference. Mary only knew that bloodletting would be in progress either way. She learned from two elderly slaves guarding the village that an Ifako chief's wife had died, and the whole village had gone to celebrate her entry into the spirit world. It would be several days before they returned. She asked where she might find shelter and they directed her to a ramshackle hut, bringing water at her request, along with wood and hot cinders to make a fire. Then they disappeared.

Mary stripped off the children and tried to infuse some warmth into them, then heated some food on the fire, all the time wondering what was keeping Bishop from turning up. He at the other end was waiting for assistance from Ekenge, for without a guarantee of safe conduct both bearers and paddlers refused to step on Okoyong territory. When he eventually arrived carrying bedding and provisions, he found the children huddling together for warmth on the mud floor of the hut, while Mary attempted to dry their clothes. She almost exploded on learning of the crew's rebellion, and set off in high dudgeon for the landing beach, leaving Bishop in charge. To her surprise, a young slave ran after her and offered to light her way, the first spontaneous act of kindness shown since her arrival.

She found the canoe moored out of reach of attackers and battened down for the night, with its occupants obviously asleep. This further fuelled her anger and, charging into the water breast-high, she began battering on the tarpaulin, scaring everyone out of their wits. Discovering her in this frame of mind and afraid of what misfortunes she might call down upon them, the crew jumped smartly to attention, loaded goods on their heads and scurried down the path towards

Ekenge at top speed. At this moment, fear of the forest and the Okoy-ongs were nothing compared with Mary's wrath.

She had charged out barefoot, her feet too swollen to force boots on again, and they were now lacerated and bruised, and infinitely more painful without her anger to spur her on. Altogether it was an unpromising start to a questionable future. Later she said, 'Had not Mr Bishop come with us, I don't know what I would have done .... The next day was the Sabbath ... miserable because it was a wet and idle one'. The misery was compounded by it being unmarked by any act of group worship, and the need to observe it meant waiting another day before anything more could be done. With time to reflect on the wisdom of coming to such a place, her spirits had seldom been lower.

The following morning the bearers worked at high speed to offload the rest of Mary's belongings before the Okoyongs appeared on the horizon. When all was piled up around her, Bishop left with reluctance, although the others, much as they revered their Ma, found staying alive had become an urgent priority. After their departure, Mary 'looked helplessly on day after day at the rain pouring down on the boxes, bedding and everything', for the hut was already full to overflowing.

Later in the week the tribe began to weave its way homeward, but Chief Edem was in no state for formal welcomes, although he did provide Mary with a better hut, next to his harem, before everyone set off again for another funeral celebration. The rain had abated, so Mary, who always maintained there were no drones in her household, no doubt allocated the children the task of transferring some of her belongings. Next she dug a latrine and erected rough fencing for privacy on the ground allocated beside Edem's compound. Then she waited once again for the tribe's return.

After they finally arrived home, the first incident to upset her was seeing the lad who had lit her way back to the landing place being dragged into a circle, where a pot of oil was boiling. Until ladles of the scalding liquid were poured over his hands and he screamed in agony, Mary had no idea what was taking place. In fury she turned on a chief who blandly told her this was his punishment for wilfully

breaking Egbo law by absenting himself from the Ifako funeral celebration. It was the Okoyong equivalent to a rap on the knuckles. She
was haunted by the suspicion that she had unwittingly played a part
in his punishment, for he had been seen accompanying her back to
the river, perhaps interpreted as a sign that he was transferring his
allegiances. At this stage there was nothing she could have done to
prevent his punishment. She could only be thankful she was allowed to
treat his burns.

Mary endured the same performance that she had experienced in
Ibaka with all the wives crowding around her, fascinated by this strange
red-haired white woman. However, she eventually succeeded in
convincing them that she would actually prefer to sleep with only her
children for company, and during the days worked at clearing the
proposed mission land when she needed quietness. Chief Edem's sister,
Ma Eme, actively sought her out, and Mary discovered she was as
anxious as herself to see an end to the bloodshed decimating the tribe.
She promised her support, provided she wasn't expected to forsake
her own customs and gods. An intelligent and shrewd woman, she
counselled Mary to tread carefully till the tribe became accustomed
to her, otherwise she might end up being killed. Mary trusted her
instinctively – and time would prove her right. It was the first glimmer
of hope since her arrival.

Having recently survived a frightening ordeal when her husband
died, Ma Eme had good reason to wish for an end to human sacrifice.
Suspected, along with her husband's other wives, of being responsible
for his death, custom dictated that she took a white fowl to her trial
and the direction in which it ran after being beheaded determined
her guilt, or in her case her innocence. After she escaped being buried
alive, Ma Eme had to submit to a period of near-starvation in widowed
seclusion until Edem used his influence to have her released.

Edem himself reminded Mary of a troublesome adolescent whom
his older sister, in the absence of a matriarchal figure, called to order
when he stepped out of line. This he frequently did, particularly with
his wives, whom he often abused when he was drunk. Living next to

his harem, Mary was made painfully aware of this, and blessed Ma Eme on many occasions when she intervened. Yet later Mary would discover Edem had his chivalrous moments. On learning that a notorious band of women, as fierce as any warriors, was going to target Mary in search of the bounty every white woman was reputed to have, he remained sober and kept watch over her hut all night, alongside his guards. Such a remarkable act of self-discipline impressed teetotal Mary greatly. However this memorable moment was still to come.

At first, bearing Ma Eme's advice in mind, she moved quietly within the community, dispensing medicine, administering first aid, and making friends with women and children who had never had a stranger, or perhaps anyone, concerned for their well-being before. It took longer to gain the confidence of the chiefs – including Edem. Suspicion was too integral a part of their make-up for it to be otherwise. The first real step forward came when Edem, belatedly concerned for a wife whose arm he had bitten during a funeral orgy, turned to Mary for help after it became badly infected. Earlier administrations by witch doctors had proved ineffectual. Mary applied disinfectants and poultices along with commonsense and the infection was quickly cured, which earned Edem's gratitude – and presumably his wife's – and also impressed the rest of the chiefs. Mary said afterwards:

> From this my fame spread far and wide, for the lady is of gentle birth and every trifling act of courtesy, I have since found, was retailed and appreciated, proving that, with all their faults, they are not insensible to kindness …. After this I had many visitors from the interior towns some of whose names were familiar as the terror of Calabar, but everyone was gentlemanly and gracious, everyone laid aside his arms at the entrance to our yard, and everyone gave us an invitation to spend a week or two at his place.

What could be more civilised than this? Such an account, straight from the pen of a down-to-earth person such as Mary, gives pause for thought. And the lady of gentle birth? Documented authentication by

Major Sealy King in the 1930s, of the Okoyong's long and proud lineage, would confirm what Mary had believed all along.

She was brought down to earth shortly afterwards. When a number of women, some of them nursing infants, were chained in Edem's yard to await trial by poison bean and left all day in the heat without food or water, she initially resisted interfering. However at night, when they were left unguarded, she ventured to take them food and was heartened to find several of Edem's wives giving them water while others kept watch. Had they been caught, they would have been flogged to death for interfering with prisoners – and possibly Mary with them.

Shortly afterwards she was allowed to attend the trial of a slave accused of enticing the concubine of one of the chiefs. From the Ibo tribe, noted for their fine looks and intelligence, the girl was considered a valuable commodity, but had eyes only for a common slave. That he had spurned her advances was of no account, and the man was sentenced to flogging, followed by execution. Mary, now seemingly accepted by the tribe, decided she had remained on the sidelines long enough, and jumped up to protest at the injustice of the sentence.

'The man has done no wrong. What else could he do but walk away from her?' She was told his punishment was for using sorcery to enchant the girl. It was obvious that the chief would settle for nothing less than blood, for the slave girl had subsequently hanged herself, so as well as losing face he had lost a beautiful and expensive concubine. Still Mary persisted. 'What evidence was there that the man had bewitched the girl?' Increasingly angered by her interruptions, the chiefs shouted that they needed no evidence – it was obvious that the slave had bewitched the girl.

'It is not obvious,' replied Mary. 'A court of law could not condemn a man to death without evidence.' But they had heard enough from this white woman accepted on sufferance, who knew nothing of their customs. Chiefs and freemen alike exploded with rage, brandishing their weapons threateningly in her face. In an oversimplification of her danger, she said later that 'things got critical'.

As angry as themselves she stared them out, eyes blazing. Eventually they quietened down, nonplussed by her apparent lack of fear, and backed off to give the matter some thought. It was decided that a mere woman could only act in this way with the power of her God behind her, so it might be prudent to let her speak. After much persuasion on Mary's part, the man's punishment was reduced to flogging alone, and she formally thanked the chiefs for showing mercy. However, to remind her they were still in charge, they ordered the man to be chained up near her hut where he was flogged mercilessly for three days in succession. When Mary felt she could bear his screams no longer, he was suddenly released and only then was she able to help him. By this time it was almost too late. At a price she had discovered she had the power to influence the tribe, and for once she was in accord with them. Without her God behind her she believed it would not have been possible.

The clash of wills between the chiefs and Mary quickly faded from the tribe's consciousness and the victim slowly recovered, thanks to Mary's administrations. That he had recovered at all she considered a miracle. Her schools in both Ifako and Ekenge had since been established, but there was no word of her promised mission house, despite reminders on her part. However she was gratified by the initial response to 'Book' in both places. The mornings were occupied by treating ailments and dispensing medicine, but each afternoon she held lessons in Ifako, while in Ekenge classes were held in Edem's yard in the evening, when wives and slaves were free to attend:

They make a motley crowd bound and free, male and female, young and old, all crammed into the shed. The master (Edem)and his sister (Eme) who can claim a pedigree few can claim in this land are hustled by the slaves bought but yesterday and there is a great deal of merriment and good nature and a great deal of earnestness in their struggle to master the alphabet and the multiplication table.

Such basics were essential for future trading with other tribes, which she was determined to encourage. After the adults gained a smattering of knowledge the attendance figures levelled out in both Ekenge and Ifako – where the chiefs, although initially uncooperative, were becoming more enthusiastic. Despite the short distance between both places, Mary was always given an armed escort, and knowing none of their people was allowed to travel without protection, she correctly interpreted this as an indication of her growing acceptance.

She introduced Christianity to them gradually, but although they sang with great enthusiasm, the concept of a God who loved everyone, whether bond or free, in equal measure, seemed beyond their comprehension, and not one the chiefs appreciated. However, the concern she consistently showed for the well-being of all played a large part in winning their confidence. Her mastery of the language and her quick-witted humour also helped. They decided that allowing the white God into their lives was doing no harm, and slotted Him in alongside His contenders. The tribe listened earnestly to Mary, and became eager to please, but were too thirled to their own beliefs to forsake them easily. Surprisingly she understood this stance, despite her evangelical aspirations and her own uncompromising beliefs. Although Mary originally had referred to the Africans' 'heathen practices', she was coming to realise that her religion and theirs had a common base, an all-powerful God they called Abasi.

Her next serious confrontation with the chiefs and Egbo was infinitely more dangerous than the first, for it took place in the evening when most of them were drunk. Mary, alerted by the Egbo drums, rushed out to learn that the chiefs, fearing her interference, had withheld knowledge of the trial of a freeman's wife, and retribution was about to take place. Apparently a slave had done some work for the woman's husband and demanded payment, intimidating her so much that she had paid him in kind with half a yam to get rid of him. In doing so she had broken the moral code by giving another man food in her husband's absence. This was witnessed and interpreted as the prelude to adultery.

Hearing the woman scream, Mary pushed to the forefront of a crowd inflamed by drink and lusting for blood, and found her staked to the ground, awaiting her punishment. Masked and painted Egbo warriors gyrated around the victim, while another stood at the ready to pour boiling oil over her naked body. The urgency of the situation made Mary suppress her recoil of horror. Slowly and deliberately, she approached the man detailed to carry out the sentence, placing herself between him and the figure spreadeagled on the ground. The crowd held its breath and waited. His response was to swing a ladle of burning oil menacingly in her direction, almost a re-run of the episode in Dundee years before with the swinging chunk of lead.

Nearer and nearer he came with the ladle but she stood her ground, her eyes fixed steadily upon him. Finally he broke and backed away in fear, while the chiefs exchanged uneasy glances and a ripple spread through the spectators. Such a show of strength from a white woman was undeniable proof that her God was a force to be reckoned with. When Mary approached Edem to intercede on the prisoner's behalf, the matter was of secondary importance compared with what had been witnessed. The woman was released into her custody and the incident was never referred to again. That night she gave thanks for the special power she had been given, and marvelled at being protected in such an amazing way.

Chapter 6
The Power of Witchcraft

A DELEGATION from a village many miles away in the direction of the Cross River arrived unexpectedly bearing gifts of four brass rods (worth approximately a shilling in trading currency) and a bottle of gin. They had travelled all day to get there, for they believed their chief was dying and had heard that the white woman might be able to save him. Mary was obviously a last resort, witch doctors having given up on him. Both Edem and Eme were strongly opposed to her making the journey into such dangerous territory, a spurious argument given the Okoyong's own reputation. They also pointed out that if the chief died she could be held responsible.

Nevertheless Mary felt she had no choice, knowing that ritual killings would follow such a death. Her main problem was failing to establish precisely what was wrong with the chief. Edem, while unable to stop her, was adamant that she be given an armed escort and many hours were wasted waiting for its arrival. For her to go under the protection of the delegation was too simple a solution, for Edem, in a desire to procrastinate, demanded proof of honourable intent.

As a result, the following day Mary had two sets of escorts: one of several freewomen who arrived to collect her; and another of warriors armed to the hilt, who waited at the edge of the village. How much this reassured her has not been recorded. However she had donned her own armoury, full missionary regalia (a rare spectacle by this time), and clutching her only weapon, a bagful of medicine, set out in pouring rain with umbrella and head held high. Before long, both hat and umbrella were cast impatiently aside, followed by her ankle-length skirt and petticoat which made progress through vast tracts of swampland almost impossible. By the time she had negotiated gullies and squelched through dripping forests, Mary was battling on barefoot in her underwear. The women stuffed her clothing into calabashes, but she held on grimly to her medicine bag.

On entering the village at last, she salvaged the remnants of her dignity with rags hastily borrowed while her own clothes were dried out. She found the tribe silent and full of apprehension and prayed hard that the chief's illness might prove to be something straightforward which a liberal dose of salts or poulticing could cure. A patient's fear of witchcraft, on which unscrupulous witch doctors traded to settle old scores, was so great that all illness was attributed to evil forces at work and even minor ailments could be considered life-threatening. Everything depended on this being the case, for if the chief were beyond help there would be few winners.

Mary never revealed what was actually wrong with him, perhaps reluctant to admit that she had left a simple but effective remedy behind. To return to Ekenge was out of the question, but she remembered there was a well-stocked dispensary at the mission station at Ikorofiong, on the other side of the Cross River. She asked if it was possible to get there. It was, but no one was prepared to risk it, instead pointing her in the direction of a Calabar trader living in his canoe on the river, who after much persuasion agreed to act as messenger. The Ikorofiong missionary, Alexander Cruickshank, whose station ran with the precision of an army garrison, no doubt marvelled that Miss Slessor had become embroiled in such a situation, but he rose to the occasion and also sent tea as a goodwill gesture. Thus fortified, Mary nursed the chief carefully throughout the night, and by the end of the next day he was well on his way to recovery.

There was universal rejoicing and justifiable acclaim for the white woman who had put her own life in jeopardy to save their chief and secure their own deliverance. Mary, on the other hand, was conscious of the teamwork which had rescued the situation, and sent up a special prayer of thanksgiving. In an upsurge of gratitude the villagers crowded around her, eager to learn about the white God and 'Book', and, reluctant to miss such an opportunity, she promised to send a teacher when possible. Stoically she set out on the long journey home-wards, staggered into Ekenge and collapsed. The fever she had been fighting, triggered by many hours of exposure to the rain, had taken hold and she took days to recover. Fortunately her children, whom she had left under supervision, were quite capable of fending for them-selves. Her success with the chief was relayed from village to village and like Chinese whispers it grew with the telling. It also played its part in her growing acceptance throughout the whole area.

Mary was discovering life in Ekenge was like being on a perpetual rollercoaster. Just when she seemed to be travelling along smoothly, it took a terrifying downward swoop. Edem's confidence, which she had been building up steadily, was suddenly lost overnight, and the conse-quences were likely to be far-reaching. He had developed a nasty abscess which had yet to respond to Mary's treatment and in a combi-nation of impatience and fear, unknown to her, he had called in a witch doctor. When she went to treat him one morning as usual, the first sight to alert her of this was a chicken impaled on a stick at the entrance. Bedecked with a selection of charms, Edem's mood was dark with foreboding as he greeted her balefully. He said someone had deliberately willed this illness upon him, and when she ridiculed the idea he angrily showed her the proof – an assortment of lead, teeth, bones and eggshells which he maintained the witch doctor had extracted from his back. He announced that there was nothing more she could do for him, then issued an order for several hostages to be chained up to await punishment. Deaf to Mary's entreaties, he informed her he was being taken to one of his farms outside Ekenge to escape her interference and would have a guard mounted to keep her out.

He was true to his word, and powerless to help. Mary spent days in agonised suspense awaiting the outcome. Under the administrations of the witch doctor his condition could only deteriorate. Ma Eme, who had proved helpful on many occasions, had departed with Edem, and hadn't been seen since. When Mary learned that more hostages had been taken, she prayed harder than ever. Then one night messengers arrived from Edem's farm requesting a letter for the missionary at Adiabo, further downriver, who was reputed to be skilful at treating ailments. Mary scribbled off a note explaining the situation, but on discovering witchcraft was involved, the missionary, an Efik convert, took fright and withheld his assistance. Fortunately his sister was prepared to go in his place, and under her care the abscess broke and Edem's sanity was restored.

In an effort to redeem himself in Mary's estimation, he sent word that all the prisoners had been released unharmed apart from one worthless slave woman who had been sold to the Inokon, a cannibal tribe. Despite knowing already that the woman had been murdered, Mary had to remain silent to protect her informers. W P Livingstone described the days which followed:

> When the chief was convalescent it was announced by drum that he would emerge on a certain day from his filth – for the natives do not wash during illness – and that gifts would be received. His wives and friends and slaves brought rum, rods, clothes, goats and fowls, and there ensued a week of drinking, dancing and fighting, worse than Mary had yet seen.

It seemed as if the whole place had erupted in madness, after the build-up of fear over the previous days, but Mary's concern that the fighting would escalate into widespread violence in this instance proved to be groundless.

Fear dominated the lives of the Okoyong on a permanent basis and she found it to be at the root of most of their troubles. She was beginning to understand the complexity of the people around her, and although the defection of their chief had upset her greatly it shouldn't have surprised her. Their belief in witchcraft went hand-in-hand with fear of evil spirits, sorcery and accusations of sorcery, of ghosts of ancestors, twins, the poison bean and of the world in general. In many instances they had reason to be afraid, as the innocent victims of convoluted plots or merely because they were in the wrong place at the wrong time. Their hold on life was precarious at the best of times, and could be severed in an instant. It only took the untimely death of a prominent figure for all hell to be let loose. Mary had seen for herself where accusations of sorcery could lead; soon she was to witness the power of inanimate objects to reduce intrepid warriors to a state of abject terror.

She had decided to escort a visiting chief and his entourage on their homeward way, aware that in their intoxicated state they were likely to cause trouble when passing a nearby township. The chief, having already crossed swords with her, only submitted to this indignity because he was too drunk to care. The men were steered safely past the settlement and were making unsteady progress without incident when they caught sight of a plantain sucker, surrounded by a coconut shell and palm leaves, which appeared to have been deliberately placed in their path. This was *ju-ju* (a West African fetish) at its worst, a dire warning of death to all who passed by, and one which transfixed the bold chief and his companions to the spot. Then, shaking with fear and rage, they took off in the direction of the township they had passed, weapons at the ready and tumbling over themselves to find the perpetrators.

Surer of foot and more familiar with the terrain, Mary managed to bypass them, and was standing calmly blocking their path as they charged blindly towards her. There was something about her stance which halted them in their tracks – already spooked, they may have thought this was a more powerful ju-ju they were up against, of the white variety. Whatever the reason, they allowed themselves to be turned around and after considerable effort Mary succeeded in leading them back to the point where the offending plantain lay. She picked it up to reassure them of its harmlessness, and laughingly said she would take it home and plant it. However they gave her and it a wide berth, while she watched to assure herself that they were travelling home in the right direction.

The next day saw a demand for the return of the plantain which was required as evidence after a witch doctor had allegedly removed a mixture of bones, teeth and suchlike from the visiting chief's person.

Already a young man from Edem's territory had been named as the guilty party and taken prisoner, and to prevent the situation developing Mary set off to plead for his release. The chief, despite actually believing she had saved his life by removing the ju-ju from his path, played cat and mouse with her, taking delight in her humiliation, but she gritted her teeth and persisted. Satisfied at last he agreed to consider the matter, but only at the eleventh hour, as Edem's forces were preparing for attack, was the hostage finally released.

Chapter 7
'The Civilising Influence of that Admirable Lady, Miss Slessor'

MARY'S promised mission house had eventually materialised after she threatened to shame Edem by building it herself. Living next to a harem, within sight and sound of all kinds of sexual activity, had been an exceedingly rough baptism for her. It was the custom for visiting chiefs to be given the hospitality of the harems, and while her cheeks burned at the shameless behaviour, what vexed her most was that slavewomen had no choice in the matter. The more valuable wives were safely locked up out of harm's way. To those who later extolled the innocence of the Africans, she tartly suggested that they tried living for a month in one of their harems.

Her two-roomed house was made of mud and wattle, with a roof of palm leaves extending in front to make a verandah, and storerooms protruding at each end. Lining the walls of the living room were bunks made of clay, and the other room where she slept – often with a child in her bed – held her portable organ, sewing machine and books. She called this home her caravan and was delighted by it, with its proper doors and windows brought from Creek Town. The women stroked her modest possessions enviously, and she encouraged their acquisitiveness, knowing they would put pressure on their men in regard to outside trading, which would benefit everyone. David Livingstone had found legitimate trade was the answer to the traffic in slaves; Mary believed it would serve equally well in reducing the drunkenness at the root of many of the Okoyong's problems. She pointed out to Edem that to trade with Calabar would work to their advantage, with their plentiful supply of palm oil and farm produce. However, he only grinned. 'We do so already, Ma. We trade in heads.' Nothing daunted, she contacted some Calabar traders, guaranteeing their safety if they would bring up a selection of their wares. But she had no takers. Following this rebuff she wrote:

> *Okoyong is a very dark tribe. They are the princes of drunkards, and smash and hash at each other and all and sundry as none of the other tribes would do. Calabar people are so frightened of them that to ask anyone to come and see us is to bring a volley of abuse or laughter down on your head .... They would as soon think of going to the moon as going to Okoyong ....*

In the meantime Ifako had followed Ekenge's lead and started work on a church, also of mud and wattle, which would double up as a school. Mary supervised its building and King Eyo sent up over a thousand palm mats to roof it. Over several days women transported the mats on their heads from the landing stage, covering twelve miles each round trip, while others smoothed the mud floor, stained walls and fashioned and polished clay benches for the congregation. Mary requested that no slaves should be employed, and all the work was undertaken by freewomen who delighted her with their enthusiasm. A box of second-hand children's clothes from Scotland had been delivered with the mats, so for the first service 'each child was radiant in some sort of garment', although most of the parents were 'dressed in their own clean skin'. For Mary the best show of their appreciation was that none of them was unwashed.

With the church up and running she renewed her efforts to change attitudes towards trading, which only relaxed when they needed arms or alcohol. The chiefs were reminded that the good life their counterparts in Calabar enjoyed had been achieved largely through trade, and she extolled the virtues of King Eyo, who was eager to help them. She decided to ask him to invite them for a visit, which would increase their confidence and whet their appetites for the benefits which could be theirs. He responded at once and after long deliberations the chiefs made ready for the adventure of their lives.

Their departure was not without incident. They had arrived at the landing stage fully armed, ignoring Mary's stipulation that weapons must be left behind. Despite their protests that she would make women of them all, she insisted on all arms being handed over to the wives seeing them off, with the result that only Edem and one other were prepared to proceed. Then the canoe, loaded with some of their finest produce, capsized the moment the two chiefs stepped aboard, surely an indication that the river god was opposed to their journey. This was nonsense, said Mary. All they needed was a bigger boat which should be loaded more carefully. While this was accomplished, she coerced three other chiefs into changing their minds and finally the larger canoe was ready to depart. Moving some cargo for better distribution, she suddenly spotted more weapons hidden away, at which point her legendary 'Carrots' temper erupted. To a stream of abuse directed at cowardly, treacherous and ungrateful chiefs whom she was wasting her time trying to help, guns and swords were flung ashore one by one, making onlookers scatter to avoid decapitation. Then she dug a paddle ferociously into the water, giving the others no option but to follow.

King Eyo, having warned his henchmen well, had ensured the Okoyong visitors a courteous reception, and they were recompensed for their goods in generous fashion. Disarmed by his kindness, and envious of the luxury he enjoyed, they agreed to further trading, and in disputes formerly resolved by bloodshed to defer to him for arbitration. Mary had been steadfastly working towards this, and that Eyo was able to bring it about was a particular source of satisfaction. The visit was rounded off by a service to which they were invited, where Eyo gave the address. He chose as his text, 'To give light to them that sit in darkness and in the shadow of death; to guide our feet into the ways of peace'.

The chiefs returned with plenty to think about, not least the esteem in which their Ma was held by King Eyo and indeed throughout Creek Town. In new appreciation of her worth, they decided to extend her existing two-roomed abode into a dwelling to rival the best houses in Calabar, and the following morning Mary was astonished to find a work party already assembled outside her yard.

Meanwhile, back in Edinburgh, one Charles Ovens was visiting an old friend, who had read in the *Missionary Record* that Miss Slessor was looking for a carpenter to assist in building her new mission house in the Okoyong. Ovens, a wandering spirit, recently returned from America, had the necessary qualifications and sense of adventure which made him respond promptly to the request, little knowing what lay in store for him.

He and Mary, sharing a similar background and sense of humour, hit it off from the outset. Practical and efficient, one of his first jobs was to finish off the church in Ifako, which still lacked doors and windows. He had a fine voice, and in the evenings with the children gathered around he would lead them in singing the old Scots songs which Mary loved. The villagers came to listen, and even Ovens' African assistant, Tom, was affected. 'I don't like these songs,' he said. 'They make my heart big and my eyes water.' Mary knew exactly what he meant.

As a result of the Calabar trip, new buildings were springing up everywhere. The latest was for Edem's son Etim, who was building his first home. In the forest one day, cutting logs to support his new roof, he was struck by a branch on the back of his neck, a freak accident which had disastrous results. He briefly regained consciousness and Mary watched anxiously as his condition deteriorated. Ovens looked on in amazement as fear stalked the whole community and accusations of sorcery flew in every direction.

Loud wailing outside sent her flying to Etim's bedside. With a witch doctor in attendance, the unconscious boy was being supported as smoke was blown into his nostrils and pepper rubbed into his eyes, while others pressed open his mouth or shouted into his ears to assist his recovery. Predictably it had the opposite effect. The cry then went up that sorcerers had killed him and the witch doctor was called to apportion blame. At this point there was a mass exodus, and instructions were given to ransack the nearest village to where Etim had been working and bring back its occupants in chains. Fortunately all but a dozen had already fled.

Mary's subsequent behaviour made Ovens believe he had stumbled into a nightmarish version of *Alice in Wonderland*. With permission from Edem, she prepared the boy's body, carefully dressed it in a smart European shirt and suit from the mission box, and wrapped it in yards of brightly coloured silk. Then she ordered his head to be shaved into intricate patterns and painted yellow, before she wound a silk turban around it, topping it all with a large black and scarlet hat, plumed with brilliant feathers. She stepped back to inspect her handiwork before the body was carried into the yard where it was placed in an armchair under a large striped umbrella.

She asked one of Edem's wives to tie a whip and the silver-topped chief's cane to the young man's hands, then placed a large mirror before him, to show him he had been dressed in appropriate style for entry into the spirit world. On a table beside him were placed the skulls he had taken in battle, his armoury and other prized possessions, along with a few lighted candles Mary had added for special effect. Edem was delighted with the result, while the people who came to view had never seen such a magnificent corpse before.

Mary's intention was to give the lad such a fine send-off that no human sacrifice would be necessary. Unaware of this, Ovens wondered what on earth she was playing at. For Mary it was the deadliest game of her life. To cap it all she sent his assistant, Tom, back to Creek Town with an urgent request for someone to come up and give a magic lantern show. Later Ovens described the scene:

> ... *more than two dozen women singing him (Etim) into the other world. The yelling seems to me like fiends. Then there are about fifty men armed with swords and guns. There are twelve people in chains, three mothers with infants, and some men brought from the next village. If Miss Slessor or I leave them they will all be put to death.*

Mary and Ovens took turns in guarding them over a long period, as excitement mounted. Edem, stupified by drink, was hell-bent on a retinue to accompany his son into the next world and Mary equally determined to thwart him. When the witch doctor began preparing esere (poison) beans for the prisoners she confronted him, categorically forbidding their use and further angering Edem. One woman was unchained and led away to have the deadly potion administered secretly and Mary sprinted after her, whisking her off to the sanctuary of the adjacent mission before anyone had time to draw breath. Back within moments, she demanded that the esere bean cocktail be replaced by the Mbiam Oath, the ultimate sacred vow, to single out the guilty parties – and to silence her the chiefs agreed, aware that Etim's burial, in such a climate, was long overdue. Consequently all but three prisoners were released.

'We have done more for you than we have ever done for anyone, and we will die before we go further,' Mary was told. Nevertheless she continued to plead on the others' behalf, so enraging Edem that he threatened to burn down her house and drive her from the village. At this point Ma Eme intervened, prostrating herself before her brother to procure the release of a woman with a baby. Edem finally agreed to release the last man, but haunted that he was betraying his dead son, he grimly held on to the remaining slavewoman. Mary realised she could do no more.

The arrival of two missionaries with their magic lantern show created the diversion she had intended and, while the wonders of the world were seen for the first time by an enthralled audience, weapons were lowered and the heat went out of the situation. Later that night, to her intense relief, the slavewoman appeared at the mission house, half-dead and still manacled, having claimed to have broken out of her chains. Mary would always maintain that Ma Eme was responsible for her release.

Preparations then went ahead for the burial under the chief's house, and for the first time in the history of the Okoyong only a cow, a striped umbrella and a mirror, along with his memorabilia, accompanied one of high rank into his grave. And when the worst of Edem's grief was over and sanity returned, he would kneel at Mary's feet to thank her and confess that he was weary of many of the old customs. That the

Above: Mary Slessor in Calabar with a group of women and children.

Below: King Eyo VII's State Canoe.

Right: Mary with the people of Ekenge.

Below: King Eyo VII of Creek Town.

Left: The Ekenge mission house built by Charles Ovens.

Right: Mary with some of the children of the mission in the Okoyong *circa* 1890.

Above: The First church in the Okoyong, built by the women of Ifako.

Below: Mary with Charles Ovens and William Bishop.

Left: Mary wearing an engagement ring on a visit home in 1891.

Below: Mary and Janie in Scotland during 1891.

Above: Mary and sixteen year-old Janie (Jean) in Scotland with Mary, Alice and Maggie during 1898.

Above: One of Mary's heavily annotated Bibles – every page is filled with her notes.

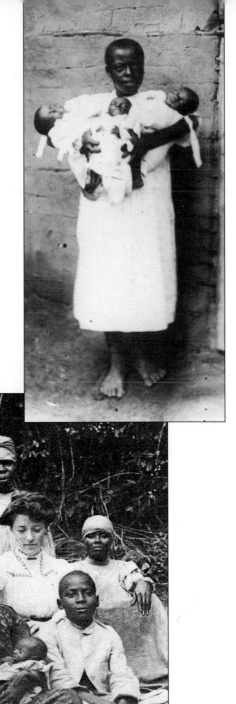

Right: Jean (Janie), Mary's 'right hand and her left' with abandoned babies.

Below: One of the last photographs of Mary's family, with an unidentified visitor.

Left: The Maltese Cross presented to Mary in 1913 by the Order of St John.

Below, left: The Mary Slessor Memorial Cross in Calabar.

Below, right: Mary's last home at Use where she died in 1915.

Bottom, right: Francis Ita Udom of Use (Ikot Oku) in Ibibio, Nigeria.

Lord should so protect her that these men put up with her interfering ways, was to Mary an ongoing source of wonder. That she had achieved such a victory against all the odds was a miracle in itself.

Yet bloodshed was not completely averted. After the funeral, fighting broke out between visiting factions and several men were killed. Egbo arrived to restore law and order and the slaves ran for cover to the mission, while villagers suspected of bewitching Etim were sought out and executed. Resenting Egbo's interference, Edem's henchmen attacked anyone found in the bush, and James Buchan describes men with whom, before Etim's death, Mary had been laughing and joking turning overnight into manic killers. It was several days before what passed as normality returned and the women and children sheltering at the mission felt safe to leave.

The chiefs began to visit Creek Town on a regular basis, finding a ready market for their goods and a generous rate of exchange, with consequent benefit to the whole tribe. They were learning to arbitrate instead of fighting and went more and more to Mary to settle their disputes. Charles Ovens succumbed to fever and Mary, who owed much to this man, nursed him in the guest-room of her new home, which exceeded all her expectations. In it she held her dispensary and school, and apart from increasing attacks of fever, which forced her to return to Duke Town to recover, she was pleased with the overall headway being made. Drinking was on the decrease, the schoolchilden were making progress and her church was well attended. Her only disappointment was the lack of genuine converts. To the accompaniment of Mary's portable organ, the large congregations sang hymns with gusto and enjoyed the sense of occasion a church service evoked, but she recognised their responses, albeit enthusiastic, had little depth. She could only sow seeds and leave the rest to God.

By late 1890 her leave was overdue, and she was seldom without fever, but while she wrote that 'no white person need fear to go anywhere now', none of her Calabar colleagues was prepared to relieve her. It was left to a recent recruit, Margaret Dunlop, to find the courage to volunteer. She arrived early and was favourably impressed by the people, although within months she would be calling them a 'wild and lawless class, boasting of their wildness', who went to church services drunk. In the meantime Edem and Eme, aware that Mary was ill, gave assurance that there would be no trouble during her absence.

To demonstrate her efficiency – an elusive quality – Mary made preparations for her departure early, which paid dividends in the light of what followed. Messengers arrived with a desperate appeal for Akamba Ma to stop a battle due to take place many miles away. It had begun with a dispute between a powerful House and a much smaller one, with the outcome a foregone conclusion. That the latter was in the wrong was no justification for its annihilation, and despite time running out, Mary felt compelled to respond.

Edem insisted on an escort and an Egbo drummer to accompany her within his territory, but she was on her own in darkness the rest of the way. Many hours later, light-headed with fever, she finally tracked down the warmongers in time to avert disaster. Whether she would be allowed the chance was another matter, being clearly the last person they wanted to see. Then suddenly Mary spotted the chief she had cured after her long wet journey over a year before. It was the breakthrough she needed, for with his backing she succeeded in arranging a palaver, where her now famous arbitration skills were put to the test. After much wrangling a settlement was reached, with a fine imposed on the offending House.

It included a payment in gin, which if consumed on the spot could spark off more trouble. But here Mary's knowledge of native customs came into play. To touch the clothes of any Egbo official was considered a violation of the official himself, and she gambled on it holding good in relation to herself. She pulled off her outer garments and flung them over the gin cases, a devise which worked like a charm, making the men draw back in angry frustration. Next she dispensed gin from a bottle out of every case to the appropriate chiefs, who had insisted on testing it for adulteration. This done, she pointed the gin-bearers firmly in the direction of home, then collapsed in an empty hut until she had recovered sufficiently to drag herself back to Ekenge.

Janie, who was travelling with Mary, greeted her with news that the Calabar launch was waiting, with their luggage already aboard. Mary made a quick change and rounded up the children who were being left in Duke Town, cutting short the usual farewells. Exhausted, she fell asleep in the launch and had to be shaken awake on arrival. However, before leaving Calabar, this past mistress in the art of surprise had time to prepare one which would rock the whole community. She sailed with a sparkling new engagement ring hidden in her luggage and two books inscribed in her suitor's hand.

Chapter 8
A Most Unlikely Vice-Consul

THAT Mary and Charles Morrison had been able to conceal their growing interest in one another was a remarkable achievement. Morrison, a fairly recent mission recruit, was responsible for training prospective African teachers, and they had first met at Mission House during one of Mary's occasional visits to Duke Town. These had become more frequent recently as she became confident she could leave the Okoyongs for short periods without all hell breaking loose. Her colleagues interpreted this as a desire to be with her own kind for a change, although she had never expressed such a wish before; with hindsight they would read into it other motives.

A gentle, sensitive man, and far from robust, Morrison seemed an unlikely suitor for Mary who, apart from bouts of fever, was robust in the extreme. But what would surprise everyone most was his age, for he was only 24, 18 years Mary's junior. When malaria forced her to spend some time in Duke Town hospital, he was a faithful visitor and their relationship had the chance to develop without the constraints of onlookers. They came from similar backgrounds and possibly part of his attraction was that he shared her love of literature, which she had discovered in Dundee and developed during long lonely periods without adult companionship. (Despite her strict presbyterian background, Mary had a surprisingly wide taste in books, which were sent regularly, along with broadsheets keeping her abreast of current events in Britain.) She may well have thought that in Charles Morrison she had met her soulmate at last, and that he was as unlike her father as one could imagine was perhaps no coincidence. Like several young men, Morrison admired her derring-do, marvelling at what it achieved, and enjoyed her mischievous sense of fun which brought a breath of fresh air into situations sorely in need of it. She was unlike any woman he had known, and her closely-cropped red hair – cut in a rebellious moment – complemented her strong features, making her look younger than her 42 years. But more important, in what mattered most they were in complete accord. When Mary returned to Ekenge they corresponded on a regular basis, and it would appear that their courtship was conducted principally in this way, otherwise it would have been common knowledge. However, they guarded their privacy jealously until their future could be resolved. Only one thing was certain – Mary would be staying in the Okoyong and Morrison was happy to go along with her.

In January 1891 she and Janie sailed into Plymouth and went straight to Topsham cemetery where her mother and sister had been laid to rest five years before. She also visited the folk who had been their kindly substitute family, finding it all a painful experience as memories flooded back. Still far from well, she followed medical advice and lingered in Devon, for Scotland seemed no longer home without her family. She preferred not to think about the prospect of addressing meetings in Morningside or Bearsden. However, by June she was back in Joppa, near Edinburgh, staying with her old friend, Mrs McCrindle, and facing up to her commitments.

Mary was a prolific correspondent and was punctilious about keeping in touch with all the churches and Sunday schools who faithfully supported her. Her regular lively letters, backed by incredible accounts of her exploits in the Okoyong brought back by missionaries on furlough, ensured an ongoing fascination with all aspects of her life. She was almost becoming a cult figure, which was the last thing she wanted, and indeed as a speaker she could be a disappointment when nerves killed all her spontaneity. On home ground she would never master the art of public speaking, and during the last few years she had had few occasions to use her native tongue, which increased her difficulties now. However, as before, she came into her own at more informal gatherings.

She had begun wearing her engagement ring publicly, and by

September both she and Morrison had informed the Mission Board in Edinburgh of their proposed marriage and their desire that Charles should join her at Ekenge. While they waited for the Board's blessing, Mary set it a second matter to consider. Provoked by a letter in the *Missionary Record* from James Luke, a colleague recuperating in Scotland, she challenged his idea that Calabar was unready for industrial training. In a strongly-worded letter she urged that the European artisans he asked for should be employed to train Africans, whom she believed had the potential to become skilled workers. She pointed out that already with a sixpenny matchet, or an ordinary hatchet, the natives made canoes, paddles, tables, seats, bedsteads, sofas, and so on:

> *Surely there are half a score of leisured men in the United Presbyterian Church who could make this matter their special business and could bring it to a practical issue. For instance, two hundred pounds would send a deputation of two, to see what the capacities of the country really are; to examine the timber, the indigenous and possible products, the water power, the character and probable cost of building, etc. They could interview the Kings, Chiefs, and other natives of influence, finding for themselves how far such work would be appreciated and supported by them ....*

For once the Board took notice, and eventually followed Mary's recommendations through, with later assistance from the British who were in the process of taking control over Calabar. In such a way the Hope Waddell Training Institute, which would train thousands of young Africans over future years, came into existence.

In her personal life Mary was less successful, for the Board decided that such a valuable asset as Charles Morrison would be wasted on Ekenge, unless a replacement of his calibre was found. No reference was made to their forthcoming marriage, perhaps an indication that it met with disapproval. Mary's response was to say, 'Poor Charlie! Pray for him', but she refused to consider joining him in Duke Town:

I could not leave my work for such a reason. To leave a field like Okoyong without a worker and go to one of ten or a dozen where the people have an open Bible and plenty of privilege! It is absurd! If God does not send him up here then he must do his work and I must do mine where we have been placed.

When he was invalided home after Mary's return, she wrote to his mother in Kirkintilloch, whom she had visited on furlough, explaining that although both were agreed that the Lord's work was paramount, should the way open the marriage might yet take place. However, Morrison never recovered sufficiently to return to Calabar, and was told to seek a drier climate. With no suitable mission post forthcoming, he ended up in North Carolina, writing in seclusion until his death shortly afterwards. In Mary's letter of condolence to his mother, she revealed for the first and only time the depth of her personal loss. She refused to discuss the matter with her colleagues, who were wise enough not to pursue it. The only other indication as to her true feelings were two books which Morrison had given her, *Eugene Aram* and *Sketches by Boz,* which she carried with her until she died.

During her absence many changes had taken place. With the recent establishment of the Niger Coast Protectorate, the British had taken over the administration of Calabar District, and Sir Claude Macdonald, the new Consul-General, was installed, with an army of three hundred soldiers garrisoned on a hill overlooking Duke Town. Proper roads and drainage had been laid and the place was clean and sweet-smelling at last. Medical and postal services were being established and launches, complete with soldiers and a Maxim machine gun, began patrolling the rivers. Vice-Consuls were appointed to administer certain districts and all was falling into place neatly, except in the territory of the Okoyong.

The Consul-General, having heard of the spectacular success Miss Slessor was having in taming this troublesome tribe, quickly sought her out on her return, to find out the tribe's likely reaction to a government official overseeing their area. Although Mary cautiously welcomed the British influence, she made it clear that the Okoyong people were not ready for it yet. She pointed out that the only reason she could mediate in their disputes was because she knew them intimately. Little did she realise that she was talking herself into a corner, and she was taken aback when Macdonald asked her to become their Vice-Consul. This was no time for impulsive decision-making, and Mary prayed hard before she finally agreed, realising no other would be tolerated.

On her arrival back at Ekenge, the warmth of her welcome left Mary in no doubt about her people's feelings for her. Eagerly, Edem told her that they had kept their promises and behaved themselves, and she believed him, although her replacements during her absence, Margaret Dunlop and a new recruit, Elizabeth Hutton, had thought otherwise. The two were back in Duke Town within a month, and only the fact that they felt duty-bound to keep faith with Mary made them return for brief visits. Good behaviour depended on one's viewpoint.

The Ekenge mission house, built from a mixture of mud and sand, had been unoccupied for several months, and was falling apart when Mary arrived, prompting her to request the help of a carpenter from Duke Town, a fellow Scot, to put it to rights. She worked alongside him, enjoying his company and his sense of the ridiculous:

> *He said as we sat at my beach one day, 'What wd the braw folk of Edinburgh think if they saw you just now?' … referring to my bare feet and very unconventional dress. He sat on the ground as I did, so I just said, 'What wd they think if they saw you?' A woollen under-garment and some unmentionables on his understandings, he looked as much a tinker as I did.*

With the departure of Charles Morrison, Mary's sense of isolation must have been acute and she was grateful for the temporary presence of a kindred spirit: 'It is splendid to have people who knew your people at home, and who can sympathise with your inclination to shout "Hallelujah" sometimes ….'

With their Ma back in control, the Okoyong knew that they had nothing to fear from the British, and accepted her new position as their Vice-Consul with equanimity. Ma Eme, who had become her staunchest ally, had her ear close to the ground, and operated a secret code to alert Mary when trouble was brewing. If an empty gin bottle arrived with a request for medicine, she prepared for action, and always seemed to turn up at the crucial moment to thwart the mischief-makers. This confirmed their belief that she had magic powers, never realising that they emanated from Eme on occasions.

Determined to put a stop to continual fighting between two Houses, Mary convened a palaver (a meeting) of all the chiefs in the area, which lasted well into the night before an acceptable agreement was reached. To ratify it, a sacred native oath was called for, when the heads of the two warring Houses knelt before her while the senior chief cut the backs of their right hands which they clasped together. Then a mixture of salt, pepper and corn was laid over the cuts until soaked in blood, which each man sucked from the other's hand. Mary respected this ancient ceremony, and knew the peace would be faithfully kept. It was a ritual in which she would take part time and again. Contrary to general opinion, some missionaries had an empathy with native beliefs and customs, and Mary had Hope Waddell, the mission's founder, who was enlightened before his time, as an example. But such individuals were few. However, James Luke's account of a chief's concern for him during an severe attack of fever is worth recording. When it appeared that the Christian God was unable to relieve him, the chief called on his own gods to to help his white friend:

> *In imperious tones he ordered me to stretch out my hand. I did so. On the back of the hand he made mysterious markings with coloured chalk ... then standing there the priestly chief poured out the libation of wine and prayed – the heathen for the Christian who sorely needed prayer. I greatly respected the heathen chief at that moment .... One other bit of common ground – praying ground; one other elementary principle of true religion – prayer for one another ....*

Mary's idea of court procedure was not what the British had in mind, but she had been given free rein to administer as she saw fit and dispensed her unique form of justice much in the manner she had presided over palavers. T D Maxwell, the Police Magistrate at Calabar and later Justice of the Supreme Court (who became a particular friend of Mary's), on his first visit to the Okoyong Native Court found her swaying gently in a rocking chair, a baby on her knee and a lace shawl draped over her hair. She looked the epitome of serenity. Then suddenly she jumped up, the shawl fell off, and the baby was thrust into someone's arms. She charged for the door where a native stood watching, seized him by the scruff of the neck, boxed his ears and hustled him out into the yard, warning him what would happen if he showed his face again without her permission. Then she returned, retrieved her shawl, picked up the baby, and began gently rocking again. Her wrath had been ignited because the man, a well-known troublemaker, had defied the ban placed upon him. One decision Maxwell recalled he often wished he could follow as a precedent:

A sued B for a small debt. B admitted owing the money and the court (Ma) ordered him to pay accordingly: but she added, 'A is a rascal. He treats his mother shamefully, neglects his children, only the other day he beat one of his wives with quite unnecessary vehemence ... his farm is a disgrace, he seldom washes, and then there was the palaver about C's goat a month ago. Oh, of course A didn't steal it, he was found not guilty, wasn't he? – all the same the matter wasn't satisfactorily cleared up, and he did look unusually sleek just about then. On the other hand B was thrifty and respectable, so before B paid the amount due he would give A a good sound caning in the presence of everybody'.

Maxwell maintained no other court he had known better deserved to be called a 'Court of Justice', although sometimes, like Shylock, the litigants got more than they desired.

Whatever her methods, Mary succeeded in bringing law and order to the Okoyong, where the inevitable changes wrought by the British were felt least of all. She guided her people through the bewildering adjustment period of co-ordinating their customs with the new laws without fuss, so that little was heard of her achievements. However, they didn't go entirely unnoticed and government officials were instructed to visit Miss Slessor to see how things should be done.

The woman they found was shabbily dressed and the direct opposite of the prototypal missionary. She had a blatant disregard for every health rule in the book, neither protecting her head from sunstroke, nor her feet from jiggers (tropical fleas which burrowed under toenails), and never used mosquito nets nor anything else guaranteed to make life more bearable in this godforsaken land – a term she would have hotly disputed. But gradually some recognised what she was about, witnessed her strength and fell under her spell. Others took her at face value and wondered what all the fuss was about.

By 1894 Mary knew she must take action to prevent the killings she no longer had time to prevent. No one was ever slaughtered in her presence, but she could only be in one place at a time. The matter came to a head when she was trying to prevent bloodshed during a twin birth in one village and the poison ordeal was about to be administered in another. For the first time she reluctantly called on the Consul-General to reinforce her authority. A Vice-Consul from Duke Town duly arrived with a guard of honour who marched smartly through the market place. They came to attention outside the mission house where Mary sat astride the roof with her skirts tucked inside her bloomers, replacing palm mats to stop the leaks.

'Och, there you are, laddie!' said she, not one bit put out. As a result of the meeting, the chiefs promised that thereafter twins would be given into the care of the mission and that there would be no further killing linked with witchcraft or the dead. Although Mary wasn't naive enough to think this would end all the problems, it was an important step in the right direction. And Okoyong chiefs and the British had come together in a spirit of reconciliation at last.

Chapter 9
Gain and Loss

W ITH the arrival of the British the rivers had been opened up and Mary began to have more visitors. None proved more welcome than Mary Henrietta Kingsley, an anthropologist and naturalist and a niece of the novelist Charles Kingsley. Thirty-two years old, and as much of an individual as Mary Slessor herself, she had been staying in Duke Town as the guest of the Consul-General for several months, exploring the creeks and swampland for rare specimens of fish, and delving into the mysteries of West African culture. Intrigued by Miss Slessor's unprecedented success in controlling the infamous Okoyongs, she invited herself for a visit, although usually she had little time for missionaries, scorning their assertion of moral superiority over beliefs contrary to their own. Yet, despite their vastly different backgrounds and conflicting views, the evangelist and the woman of the world became friends, recognising in each other a kindred spirit which circumvented all differences. This was confirmed in Kingsley's subsequent book, *Travels in West Africa,* in which she said the days spent with Mary Slessor were some of the most pleasant of her life.

Smartly dressed in formal attire complete with velvet toque and high-buttoned boots, she might have been 'paying a call in Kensington' had it not been for the revolver concealed in her handbag, in case things 'got too uncomfortable' on the way. She arrived during a moment of high drama, when Mary Slessor had little time for social niceties. Hearing of a twin birth in a nearby village, the missionary had dropped everything and taken off along the bush path at high speed, meeting the new mother along the way; previously well treated – as good slaves generally were – the young slave woman had been hounded out of the village after giving birth to the abomination of twins. On her head she carried a wooden box into which the unfortunate infants had been thrown, along with her few possessions and, still weak and obviously terrified, only fear of the mob in pursuit her kept her moving at all. Mary quickly took the box from her and ordered the villagers back the way they had come, flaying them with a tongue as fluent and twice as caustic as any native's.

She knew better than to return by the same route – for so great was her own villagers' fear, they would have been forced to cut another path to avoid contamination. Instead, she instructed her boys to hack a rough track through the forest to allow alternative access to the mission. Mary Kingsley recorded how Mary then 'attended with all kindness, promptness and skill, to the woman and children', but that 'all the attention one of the children wanted ... was burying, for the people who had crammed them into the box had utterly smashed the child's head'.

Mary was universally boycotted for dread of defilement from the surviving infant, whom rumour said – correctly – that she even took into her bed at night; and Edem, especially upset, declared that he could never again set foot in his Ma's house. Only after his sister Eme paid Mary a visit and people convinced themselves that the dead twin was the one spawned by the devil, did the situation improve, although they would continue to give the survivor a wide berth.

Meanwhile, with time at their disposal, a strong relationship began to develop between Mary and her visitor, who sat into the night discussing, arguing and surprisingly often agreeing on many subjects. Mary Kingsley, not given to waxing lyrical over missionaries, afterwards gave her friend the ultimate accolade:

This very wonderful lady ... her abilities both physical and intellectual have given her among the savage tribe a unique position and won her among many, black and white, a profound esteem. Her knowledge of the native, his language, his ways of thought, his diseases, his difficulties, and all that is his, is extraordinary, and the amount of good she had done no man can fully estimate ... this instance of what one white can do would give many lessons in West Coast administration and development. Only the type of man Miss Slessor represents is rare. There are but few who have the power of resistance to the malarial climate, and of acquiring the language and an insight into the negro mind, so perhaps after all it is no great wonder that Miss Slessor stands alone as she certain does.

Mary, for her part, would later defend her friend fiercely in the face of criticism from colleagues who took umbrage at Kingsley's view that missionaries exerted too much influence at home and presented an exaggerated and inaccurate picture of African life. She was even able to rationalise her visitor's attitude towards polygamy:

She would, like Mohammed, allow polygamy to work out its own ideals by its own evolution. The only fear she had for Africa's future was the tacking on, as it were, by creeds of any kind or government, or false ideas as to the dignity of labour, of a kind of spurious civilisation and a Christianity which should denationalise the race ....

Mary Kingsley returned for another visit, and although she became a recognised authority on West African culture much of the credit lay at Mary Slessor's door. The two women continued to write regularly to each other until 1900 when Kingsley died of enteric fever in South Africa while nursing Boer War prisoners. Mary mourned her deeply and paid her own tribute:

Richly gifted in humour, she could see all the Africans' follies and foolishness but she never under-rated them as a race, and there was no sting or contempt in her joke or her laugh, and what is more uncommon even among missionaries, she respected their religious beliefs however foolish.

Shortly after Kingsley's departure, hopes that inter tribal fighting was becoming a thing of the past were shattered when both Ekenge and Ifako erupted into full-scale violence. They won a battle against two neighbouring Houses and returned with some women accused of causing the trouble, who were herded into a stockade to await execution. Mary's protests and attempts at mediation this time went unheeded, but knowing no killing would take place in her presence, she instructed her girls to bring her tea and food at intervals, and settled down for a long vigil, knitting with grim determination throughout the night.

The following day a tornado forced the prisoners' guards to abandon their watch, while Mary's girls ran to inform her there was no dry bedding or clothes because the mission roof had blown off and the babies' tinned milk was running out. She found them all alternative shelter, then, praying that the prisoners would survive till her return, set off for Creek Town mission – the only source of more milk – along a forest path created when trading had begun between the two communities. While it was folly to attempt this twelve-mile journey in wind and rain and darkness, she believed she had no alternative. With her only weapon a lantern, it was fortunate that leopards, like all cats, disliked getting wet, and she finally arrived at Creek Town at four in the morning.

The astounded missionary in residence gathered her wits, along with blankets, milk and a canoe and crew, sending Mary home by river, and she was back in her place calmly knitting again before the guards reappeared. Told of this episode by the Krumen delivering the goods from the canoe, Edem groaned, recognising Ma was in fighting mode and would be prepared to sit them out. Weary of fighting, neither he nor the other chiefs could face another battle – albeit verbal – and orders were given for the prisoners' release.

Running out of milk was typical of Mary's haphazard housekeeping, so hardly surprisingly there was no rush to join her when she asked for assistance. Her duties as Vice-Consul had increased her workload, and she was constantly in demand by chiefs perplexed by the new laws and conditions laid down by the British, but this cut no ice with some mission staff who considered her Vice-Consular work inappropriate for any missionary, particularly a woman. They may also still have been smarting from her earlier wish to distance herself from them. Granted she had tamed her refractory tribe, and her courage and dedication were never in question, but her methods and lack of appropriate dignity were another matter. Her way of life was too erratic, her moods too unpredictable and her ideas of home comforts non-existent.

Much less understandable was the lack of support Mary would continue to receive from Calabar Presbytery for many years, for no ordained minister had conducted services in the church so carefully built. Admittedly Hugh Goldie (by then an old man) visited her, but apparently not in the role of a guest preacher. Whether Mary had raised hackles at some point – not inconceivable – or whether the Presbytery was suffering from lack of staff or simply sensitivity, is open to speculation. But an occasional visible presence from the Church Mary endeavoured to represent would have not gone amiss.

Following her visit to Creek Town she went down with fever and a severe attack of dysentery. Dr Robert Laws, a medical missionary who would make his name in the territory of Mary's hero, David Livingstone, visited her on a professional basis on hearing of her illness. However, he would have sought her out anyhow, having travelled from Edinburgh to look into her proposal for an industrial training centre. She staggered to the door to meet him and he took one look and promptly ordered her back to bed, becoming famous thereafter in mission circles as 'the man who made Miss Slessor do as she was told'. In his official report he afterwards wrote:

> *I could not commend her as a pattern to others, but she has saved lives as no other man or woman would have dared to do. Had a man attempted to do what she has done in the recent riot, he would have had his throat cut.*

However she had days of black depression. 'The school work is simply a scramble at the thing ... I cannot overtake it. It is because I am not doing it efficiently that I am grieved.' Yet somehow she found time to write a lengthy report summarising the results of seven years' work, in which there is a hint of her hurt and disappointment:

We do not attempt to give in numbers those who are nominally Christian. Women, lads, girls and a few men profess to have placed themselves in God's hands. All the children are sent to school without stipulation. We speak with diffidence; for as no ordained minister has ever been resident or available for more than a short visit, no observance of the ordinances of Baptism or the Lord's Supper have been held and we have not had the usual definite offers of persons as candidates for Church membership ....

Of results as affecting the condition and conduct, it is easier to speak. Raiding, plundering, the stealing of slaves, have almost entirely ceased. Any person from any place can now come for trade or pleasure ... their persons and property being as safe as in Calabar. For fully a year we have heard of nothing like violence from even the most backward of our people .... No tribe was formerly so feared because of their utter disregard for human life, but human life is now safe ....

This she attributed solely to God's answer to prayer, and marvelled that 'hordes of armed, drunken, passion-swayed men would give heed and chivalrous homage to a woman' – a seemingly exaggerated statement which was, by Okoyong standards, entirely true. It is remarkable that no man ever tried to molest Mary during all her time in Nigeria, despite the vulnerability of her situation. Only once, when she was attempting to break up a brawl, was she thrown to the ground – and this was accidental. Nevertheless, the man deemed responsible was set upon by an angry mob until Mary, unharmed, charged to his rescue.

In her report she affirmed that killings at funerals had stopped and there was a marked decline in drinking. Also there was a gradual change in attitudes towards twins since the Governor reinforced the Vice-Consul's treaty with the chiefs, although she admitted a lack of progress on the education front. She mentioned the many claims upon her and ended by asking: 'Where is the time and strength for comprehensive work of a more directly evangelistic and teaching type, specially when the station is manned year after year by the magnificent total of one individual?'

The twin girl rescued during Mary Kingsley's visit, named Susie after Susan Slessor, was now 14 months old and Mary doted on her. One terrible day this particularly bonnie child pulled a ewer of boiling water over herself and lingered between life and death for several days. Mary cradled her in her arms the long miles to Creek Town, where the doctor confirmed her worst fears. During this time a young woman from home, Miss Murray, who had answered Mary's plea for an assistant (but whose stay was brief, due to ill health) stepped in, even conducting the child's funeral when Mary, prostrate with grief, seemed incapable of doing so. Amazingly, the whole village turned out in force to mourn the death of this twin, thus supporting their Ma whose suffering affected them deeply.

The departure of Mary's assistant compounded her sense of loss and isolation; without her household of children, who made her laugh in spite of herself, she would have found it unbearable. While she cared about every waif and stray in her care, five in particular would become an intrinsic part of her family. First came Janie, the twin baptised in Dundee (who now called herself Jean), then Annie, saved by Mary as an infant from burial alongside her dead slave mother. Next there was Mary, another twin found abandoned after a week's exposure in the bush, and Alice and Maggie, some of whom would travel with her to Scotland on her next furlough. Others would add to the family later.

Despite their rough and ready lifestyle, Mary genuinely loved her bairns, although she demanded much of them, and they became self-reliant from an early age. Strict on occasions, she could also enter wholeheartedly into childlike activities. Her sense of fun would bubble up unexpectedly, a side of her character which would have confounded many. The highlight of their days was the arrival of a mission box from home which always included treats for everyone, and from this grew Mary's addiction to home-made toffee which left her toothless in years to come.

The year had been particularly difficult. First Susie died, followed by Hugh Goldie, from whom Mary had learned so much, then William

Anderson, recently returned to Calabar after a few years of unfulfilled retirement. Visiting her when she became hospitalised after working to the point of collapse, he had held her hand, recalling the young feisty spirit which sometimes had driven him to distraction, but achieved remarkable results. Weeks later Mary was at his bedside just before he died. He and Goldie were the last of the old timers, apart from Alexander Cruickshank, who remained in Calabar for a remarkable 54 years, and the equally indomitable Mammie Fuller. Mary had lost her friend King Eyo some time before and most of her early colleagues had also died or been invalided home. The turnover of mission staff because of the climate was frightening. Towards the end of the year she also lost four babies, who might have been saved had they been treated in isolation. That Hogmanay, always a melancholy time for her, was bleak indeed.

In 1896 a market had opened at Akpap, a few miles to the west, nearer the Cross river, with new farms and settlements springing up everywhere. Mary's people had worked their land out, and with more and more following Ma Eme's lead and uprooting to Akpap, she informed Presbytery that it would be necessary to consider moving the mission there. Although six miles from Ikunetu, the nearest landing place, it had the advantage of launches plying the river regularly, and the move was finally sanctioned.

Characteristically she took off at once with her brood of children, unable to wait for her new frame house to be erected. She left two of her ablest pupils to carry on the school at Ekenge and the Consul-General agreed to the transfer of her native court to the new location. She found a two-roomed mud hut, had a lean-to constructed to accommodate the overspill and settled down in conditions akin to her first home in Ekenge, with life quickly assuming its familiar pattern.

Soon the whole area was to be swept by an outbreak of smallpox, and Mary was vaccinating night and day, with Jean (Janie), now 14, assisting her in an effort to stem the outbreak. When her old friend Charles Ovens arrived with a new recruit, Mr Alexander, to assemble her new house, they found her scraping pus from the scabs of people already vaccinated and applying it to others because the supply of lymph from Calabar was exhausted.

She learned that Edem was a victim in the epidemic, now raging in Ekenge and, leaving Jean with the children, sped back to her old village, where, shocked beyond measure, she had to use her former mission house to accommodate the dying. The dead were already piled up around her. With nobody to assist her – for everyone uninfected had fled – it was some time before she discovered Edem was already dead. On the point of collapse but determined her chief should have a proper burial – for she owed him this much – she knocked up a rough coffin, then dug a hole in the earth floor deep enough to lay him to rest in dignity. She searched for his staff and whip, which denoted his rank, and buried them beside him. The village she left, to which no one would ever return, was now silent, and like her former mission house it would eventually disappear into the bush.

Chapter 10
The Aftermath of the Aro Expedition of 1901

OVENS was aware that Mary's leave, almost a year overdue, was now an urgent priority. He alerted Presbytery, offering to take her place, and since the smallpox epidemic was almost over she was persuaded to go home on the first available ship. At her own expense she was taking four girls with her, with arrangements made to house the other children in Duke Town. None of them had decent clothes for such a visit, but Mary, too weary to care, was confident that God would sort out the problem. And sure enough, His emissaries in Duke Town, the female agents, responded, appalled by the prospect of Mary letting them down. They raided the mission boxes for material and clothes to adapt, confident that the eyes of Scottish congregations would show no flicker of recognition by the time they were finished.

Mary maintained she became ill when she was idle, probably because she always worked till she dropped, which happened now, from the usual combination of exhaustion, fever and self-neglect. However six weeks' rest and decent food aboard ship helped the healing process, while Jean kept a rein on the younger children. The first indication her friend Mrs McCrindle had of Mary's impending arrival in Edinburgh was a telegram when the ship docked at Liverpool. She had no warning whatsoever regarding four extra house guests, but fortunately all Mary wanted was 'a place to hide in: away from conventionalities and all the paraphernalia of civilisation'. After a few weeks she found it in Portobello, where the family slept and ate and paddled in the sea as the notion took them. Five year-old Mary even found time to attend school there, until they were all whisked away to Bowden St Boswells, where Miss Adams, convener of the Zenana Committee – the official body now responsible for women's missionary work – took them in hand.

This philanthropic and wealthy lady settled them into one of her houses set aside for missionaries on leave, and in kindly fashion made sure they had nourishing meals and a generally more disciplined way of living. She was a good friend and liberal in supporting the missions. Therefore, earlier than she would have chosen, Mary conformed to protocol and allowed herself to be swept into the inevitable round of engagements. But she was finding it increasingly difficult to adjust to the expectations of well-heeled audiences a million miles removed in culture as well as distance from those back home – for home was now Africa. Yet she owed it to these congregations and others less affluent without whom the missions would cease to exist. The boxes of provisions and clothing – ludicrously inappropriate on occasions – with home-made goodies tucked inside, which arrived regularly, were reason alone for gratitude.

Addressing a large gathering in Scotland always unnerved Mary and celebrity status was one she seldom enjoyed – but being reunited with friends who had remained in touch was another matter. She was moved by the kindness shown to the children and overwhelmed on occasions by the continuing loyalty to herself. Less enjoyable was the notoriety into which she was about to be plunged. On her return journey there was a delay in joining the ship at Liverpool and at the quay she caught the attention of a Reuter's correspondent. Intrigued by this small woman with her brood of African children, he scented a story and drew her into conversation. Mary responded with her usual forthrightness, pleased that he seemed interested in mission work, and let slip that in the course of it she had saved over 50 pairs of twins; nice man, she thought at the time, then dismissed him from her mind. The last thing she expected was to immediately hit the headlines and become known to the public at large. The news travelled before her, and at each port of call she had to refuse invitations ashore, black-affronted that her tongue had given her away. That Christmas, spent on board, they were fêted on the grand scale, and the children returned to Akpap's spartan conditions and a diet of yams (potato-like tubers) with less than enthusiasm. Mary was just glad to get on with her life again.

With a new mission house to offer and her unruly tribe tamed, she began pressing for someone to take her place. She had long since prepared the ground for a 'proper minister', and it was time to move forward. She was particularly interested in the vast uncharted territory which lay west of the Cross River, where the Aro tribe dominated its neighbours, the Ibos and Ibibios. The Aros were reputed to be the perpetrators of unspeakable barbarity and Mary had expressed a desire to work there for some time. However, with a serious shortage of missionaries, no help was forthcoming.

Jean, now 17, was being courted by a lad who accepted without quibble that she was a twin, and Mary encouraged the match, for he was her 'ablest pupil' and she rated him highly. Unfortunately when the first child of the marriage died, the age-old stigma attached to twins returned to haunt him, convincing him that his wife was indeed accursed – which effectively ended the relationship. Jean returned to the mission, reeling from the double blow, and Mary's heart went out to her, as she sadly recognised that even among the enlightened attitudes wouldn't change overnight.

With their way of life threatened, more and more chiefs were travelling considerable distances to ask her advice about handling the British, and Mary herself was covering many miles on Vice-Consular work, apart from her other duties. Her reputation for fairness had spread outwith her own territory and when a serious dispute broke out between the Okoyong and the Umon, further up the Cross River, she was asked to arbitrate. On the return journey she had the chance to visit Itu, a market town at the junction of the Enyong Creek, which led to Ibo territory. A strong and intelligent race, the Ibos were prime targets for their neighbours, the Aros, who had grown rich over centuries of slave dealing and still used the Creek to transport their human cargo to a huge slave market at Itu. Although overseas slave traffic had stopped, internal trading continued and the trans-African slave routes were still open.

Mary knew the British were building a military base at Itu, 20 miles upriver from Ikunetu, which would inhibit the slave market and be easily accessible. She believed it would also make an ideal mission site. Its chiefs, uneasy about the British presence, begged her to make her home with them, offering her land for a school. Back at Akpap, she prayed about it and meanwhile 'drudged on', till finally she collapsed and had to be hospitalised for several weeks. She was forced to rely increasingly on Jean, who had grown closer since her return and of whom she was justifiably proud, for she was an affectionate intelligent girl and extremely competent.

Meanwhile the formation of the British Protectorates of Northern and Southern Nigeria had come into existence in 1900, when Sir Ralph Moor became responsible for the Southern Province, with a commission to explore and pacify the hinterland. He was determined to destroy the sinister power of the Long Ju-ju, an oracle situated up the Enyong Creek, at Arochuku, where Aro priests and agents controlled many hundreds of miles unknown to white men. (In 1894 Roger Casement, then a young Vice-Consul, had attempted to explore Aro territory to open up trade, but 15 miles inland he was driven back, narrowly escaping death.) The first aim was to put an end to the inland slave trade which emanated from Arochuku, but after 136 tribesmen, having travelled from near the Niger to consult the Chuku Oracle, staggered half-dead into a British post and told their story, the matter became a priority. As the only survivors out of 800, they confirmed practices of cannibalism, exploitation and enslavement so terrible that the British were forced to take action. One hundred and fifty white officers and several thousand African troops were now assembling to prepare for the Aro Expedition which would wipe the Oracle off the face of the earth, but would take more than a year to accomplish.

Prior to the launching of the British attack, all missionaries outwith Duke Town were ordered back to base for their own protection, and when Mary refused to go a military escort came to collect her. Three years after her last visit to Duke Town, she was elated to find the Hope Waddell Training Institute, her brainchild of several years before, now successfully underway. She liked the Principal, J K Macgregor, right from the start, a feeling which was reciprocated:

A slim figure, of middle height, she is no ordinary woman. It is wonderful to sit and listen to her talking, for she is most fascinating and besides being a humourist, she is a mine of information on Mission History and Efik customs.

However the 'terrible bright sky' was a problem to Mary after years of forest life, as were the army wives who seemed to have taken over the place. With the mosquito now identified as the source of malaria, health hazards were reduced and there was an increasing number of camp followers. The mission staff was saddened by the blatant race discrimination practised by the incomers and Mary, her dander up, excelled herself in outrageous behaviour, cavorting with the slaves in unseemly manner and addressing officers in broadest Dundonian. 'That coarse woman', one new missionary called her, unaware of her finer attributes.

By 24 December 1901, the Aro Expedition had achieved its purpose and, ahead of permission, Mary immediately set off for Akpap. Over several weeks messengers from distraught Aro chiefs – who knew her of old from passing through her area – managed to visit her, despite the temporary closure of the river. Frightened and resentful, they trusted only her, and many hours were spent unravelling the terms of a deal proposed by the High Commissioner. The final settlement was attributed by many as largely due to her influence.

One personal benefit from her enforced stay in Duke Town was meeting Janet Wright, one of the former Falkirk schoolgirls who had followed in her footsteps. Janet eagerly took up Mary's invitation to join her at Akpap and applied for permission at once. But due to the upheaval when the United Presbyterian and the Free Churches merged in 1900 to become the United Free Church of Scotland, communications were held up, and it was almost two years before Janet arrived in Akpap.

'She is a right sisterly helpmate and comfort in every way. Things go as smoothly as a summer's day and I don't know how I ever got on alone. It seems too good to be true.' So said Mary after nearly 15 years on her own, for Janet had adapted cheerfully to the other's ways and had taken over many responsibilities. But Mary's contentment was short-lived. Already she had settled three of her best pupils into Itu, with a school up and running, and was making regular visits to give moral support. She liked the people and the easy friendliness between the sexes, which never existed in the Okoyong:

I wish Crocket had been here to gather the shafts and sparks of wit and satire that flew with as much zest as ever obtained in a Galloway byre or a market fairin'. It is such a treat for me ... they were daffin' and lauchin' as in Scotland.

Taking advantage of Janet's presence, she decided to spend a week in Itu and set off with two boys to meet the weekly government launch at Ikunetu. Hot and tired after the six-mile walk to the beach, she sat down to recover, told the boys to keep watch, then fell asleep. She awoke to find the launch gone and two shamefaced lads standing before her. Fortunately for them she seemed unconcerned. 'God didnae mean me to go the day,' she told Janet afterwards. 'He'll hae a reason.'

The reason would soon become clear. The commander of the Aro expedition, Lt.-Col. Montanaro, was on board the launch the following week and he welcomed her warmly, knowing the reputation of this bronzed gipsy-like woman. Although she had paid lip service to formality and was wearing plimsolls, his immaculately turned out officers found her the most unlikely Vice-Consul they had ever clapped eyes on – but were warned to give her special attention. When she enquired about the current situation in Arochuku, 20 miles up the Enyong Creek, Montanaro invited her to come and see for herself, an opportunity too good to miss. She looked around in delight as they entered the Creek, serene and beautiful, with its tall tropical trees and profusion of blossoms, and a carpet of waterlilies covering its entire length. W P Livingstone described it as a place of 'fairylike enchantment'. Mary called it 'awful bonnie'. She found it impossible to associate with the scene of such former ugliness.

When the launch arrived at Amasu, the landing place for Arochuku, she recognised Aro chiefs who had visited her earlier and went over to talk to them. Her welcome baffled the British officers, who afterwards asked if she really knew these men? 'Oh aye, ah ken them fine,' she replied, omitting to say she was giving them shelter at the mission before her compatriots knew anything about them. She told Montanaro the chiefs wanted her to set up a school at Amasu, to which she had agreed, on condition that any African teacher in her absence was left unmolested. This they had promised. When Mary learned there were about 30,000 people living in forest settlements around Arochuku, and probably as many in towns along the Creek, it became abundantly clear that God was pointing her in this direction. But Amasu was over 40 miles from Akpap, and when no launch was available the journey would take at least eight hours with a good tide and considerably longer during the dry season. The crux of the matter was finding someone experienced to take over Akpap. In all conscience she couldn't expect Janet to do so.

In August 1903, to mark 15 years in the Okoyong and the culmination of her work there, Mary asked an ordained missionary to come and administer the Sacraments of Baptism and the Lord's Supper for the first time. The church was packed for this momentous occasion, but at the last minute some who had made a commitment reneged, confusing the Sacraments with the Mbiam Oath – when after drinking the vile Mbiam liquid, they believed one who falsely forswore would drop dead on the spot. In the end only eleven came forward, mostly from Mary's immediate circle. Jean brought the child she had wet-nursed and loved after her own child died, and took the vows on his behalf, bringing Daniel McArthur Slessor, called after his namesake in Scotland, into the visible membership of the Church, along with the rest of Mary's family. Despite having nothing more positive to show for 15 years of missionary work, it was one of the proudest days of her life.

Janet began accompanying her to Itu and as far as Amasu, and gave her backing to a provocative letter passed on by Calabar Presbytery (now the Mission Council) to Edinburgh:

I think it is an open secret that for years the workers here have thought our methods ... far from adequate to overtake the needs of our immense field, and as the opportunities multiply and the needs grow more clamant, the question grows in importance and gravity. The fact that only by stated consecutive work can a church be built up ... cannot be gainsaid, yet there is an essential need for something in between, something more mobile and flexible ....

Among other suggestions, Mary advocated using itinerating Africans to carry the Gospel to their fellow countrymen, a plan which Hope Waddell had introduced many years before. It had failed because of inter tribal fighting, but could work now that the British were policing the area. Her own future plans were precise:

By January 2, 1904, I shall be out five years, and so my furlough will then be due, but as I have not the slightest intention of going to Britain ... I propose to ask leave from my work at Akpap for six months, during which time I should, in a very easy way, try to keep up an informal system of itinerating between Okoyong and Arochuku.

She would find her own canoe and crew and members of her family would help to teach at elementary level, while she would be based at Itu, a vital strategic point where a school and house had already been built (which would be news to everyone). If the mission would send a companion for Miss Wright, the three of them 'could dovetail detail of the work so that no part should suffer'. She also recommended that all this should take place before the end of the year, but ended on a conciliatory note, conceding that their plans could be changed if necessary.

What Edinburgh made of it, when further expansion had been banned because of lack of recruits and financial resources, can only be guessed. But Mary's huge following within home congregations made the Foreign Mission Board tread softly. Therefore she was given permission, provided the undertaking was financed out of her own salary. Since she had already saved the mission the expense of her passage home and would never cost it another penny, it was getting a better deal than it knew.

Mary had invited Mr Wilkie, an ordained missionary at Duke Town who was in sympathy with her vision to visit Arochuku and its environs, to see for himself the opportunities unfolding, and on his return he endorsed her judgment and asked the mission to give Miss Slessor its full backing. However she was in hospital when permission came through, and it seemed unlikely that she would be going anywhere. Two months later she wrote:

I rose a mere wreck of what I was, and that was not much at the best. My hair is silvered enough to please anyone now and I am nervous and easily knocked up, and so rheumatic that I cannot get up without pain.

(The reference to her hair went back to being teased that she only went bare-headed to show off its beautiful colour.) Yet the most remarkable aspect of all Mary's illnesses was her ability to recover and fight another day. She refused to consider being invalided home, and went on with her preparations. After twelve years as Vice-Consul she relinquished her post and declined an invitation to a reception given by the High Commissioner, having neither the clothes nor enthusiasm for it. Therefore he visited her instead, pledging full support to her venture. Janet Wright was seen off on furlough and two female agents agreed to fill the empty places.

It seems strange to be starting with a family on a gipsy life in a canoe, but God will take care of us. Whether I shall find His place for me up-river or whether I shall come back to my own people (the Okoyong) again I do not know. He knows and that is enough.

Despite Mary's confidence in God's guiding hand, when her people came to say farewell the night before her departure, laden with gifts and weeping profusely, she also was deeply upset and her fever returned. Fortunately Jean was there to help, and by the time they reached Itu Mary was ready and eager for what lay ahead.

Chapter 11
The British Empire's First Woman Magistrate

HER three clever pupils had 'done wonders' at Itu, with a well-run school and a congregation waiting to greet her. But the mission house was still unfinished. However Mary had come prepared, having gathered building material and tools in Duke Town before she left. 'You're surely richer than usual in household gear,' a colleague there had remarked, watching trunks being loaded into a canoe. 'It's cement powder,' was the reply. 'There's nae bags and I'm needing it.' By now an expert in laying cement floors – to keep the fiendish driver ants at bay – she was asked who taught her the art. 'Naebody. I just mix it and stir it like porridge. Then I turn it oot, smooth it wi' a stick and say, "Lord, here's the cement. If it be Thy will please set it!" And he aye does!'

Word had spread that Ma would turn no baby away, and a visiting government doctor found her sitting in a sparsely furnished hut rocking a tiny infant, with five others lined up on the floor wrapped in brown paper. (This was unlike Mary who usually tucked her babies in blankets inside milk crates.) Later he said, 'How she managed to look after these children and do the work she does passes my comprehension'. He obviously hadn't discovered Jean, who was both Mary's 'right hand and her left'.

When Lt.-Col. Montanaro called to offer assistance, she was delighted, but less so when a deputation of young men from Akpap arrived. Apparently her two mission replacements had only lasted a month, and the Okoyong wanted their Ma back. She fed the lads and gave them shelter for the night, promising to do what she could, as indeed she did later. However there was a constant stream of chiefs arriving with problems. While the Ibibios principally needed reassurance, the Aros, resentful that their vast revenue from slave-dealing had been cut off, were seeking viable alternatives. But all were clamouring for 'Book' and God, in that order.

One exception was a wealthy chief, Onoyom Iya Nya, whose territory lay several miles up the Enyong Creek. His interest in Christianity had been awakened from a chance encounter with a renegade Calabar missionary who had earlier pointed him in Mary's direction. Onoyom was already predisposed towards missionaries, for two of them, the first white men he had ever encountered, had ventured up the Creek and saved his life as a boy. Seeking Mary out had altered his life and he was already a committed Christian. At present he was having a church built, not of mud and thatch, but of iron – like his own house. To construct the interior, he was defying the old gods and using wood from a huge tree recognised as the principal ju-ju of the village.

The whole area was in a state of flux and trade experts and British officials also sought Mary out to obtain information no other could supply, so at first she was unable to travel far afield. Yet she was drawn like a magnet to the new areas opening up. She knew missionaries of every denomination would be lining up to stake their claim and was determined to be at the front of the queue. For one so tolerant of many African beliefs, who loved Ma Eme – still holding fast to the ancient beliefs – like an 'almost sister', Mary's description of Roman Catholics as 'that corrupt body', whom she wished to forestall in the race for sectarian supremacy, seems out of character. Ingrained attitudes apparently remained, despite her enlightened views in other directions. Yet she jumped on another with similar prejudices, saying impatiently, 'They'll nae take them tae hell!'

At her first Mission Council meeting in six years, she gave a report of her progress. By this time four places along the Creek had the beginnings of congregations and schools and Mary hoped to see a native, self-supporting agency established under the control of the mission. At Amasu and Arochuku, ground had been given by the chiefs and a school was built, while at Itu the day-school was running satisfactorily and the new church held weekly services, with 40 people under Christian instruction. Mary was formally thanked and given permission to continue her self-imposed roving commission for another six months, but was reminded that no expense to the mission should be incurred. A colleague, James Luke, later put it in a nutshell: 'Where the Church has failed, a single woman has stepped into the breach ....'

Nevertheless, the Foreign Mission Board in Edinburgh had sat up and taken notice, and plans were already afoot to make Itu a medical base. A motor launch for the Creek journeys was also in the pipeline, with £400 raised by the students of New College, Edinburgh, for the purpose. Before long a hospital would be fully operational through the generosity of a Mr Kemp, of Braid United Free Church, who asked that it be called the Mary Slessor Mission Hospital. On hearing the news, Mary said it seemed like a fairytale.

When a new military and administrative centre was built 25 miles from Itu, at Ikot Ekpene, in Ibibio territory, Charles Partridge came into her life. He was appointed District Commissioner and in late December 1904 arrived at Itu with a huge Christmas pudding for Mary's family. In the first of over a hundred letters written to him over the next ten years – their main form of communication – she was almost girlish in her thanks:

Dear Mr Partridge
I can't help it! I must write a 'thank-you' for such a lovely Pudding! .... Surely it is a Home Made one and what about the basin? Am I to keep that too? for such a basin is in itself a big thing here ... I refused to let the children boil the Pudding till yesterday morning, and we had it for breakfast, tea and dinner, and again for breakfast this morning. A Plum Pudding is my weakness and it was always on the table on my birthdays (when I had a home and birthdays) ....

He dropped by at intervals and recognising her qualities encouraged her to strike out in his direction where roads were being laid. Other government officials were of the same mind. 'Get a bicycle, Ma, and come as far as you can – we will soon have a motor car service for you.' She had won the respect of men with no interest in religion and one told her that the more he saw of mission work in West Africa the less he liked it: 'Give me the genuine bushman, who respects his ancestral deities and his chief and himself .... But if all missionaries were like you ...!' Another said a pluckier woman had rarely existed, and that her strength of character was extraordinary: 'I would personally have trusted her judgment on native matters in preference to all others.' It would appear that these men appreciated her qualities more than the mission fraternity at this time.

Mary took part of the advice and walked back and forth six miles to Ikot Obong regularly, having established a school there with the help of a twelve year-old boy, after Itu prevented Ibibios from attending theirs. The demand for education was universal and, in the absence of teachers, she was often forced to use youngsters only a page ahead of their pupils. But walking long distances was becoming increasingly difficult and she greeted the arrival of Dr Robertson from Creek Town to take over Itu with some relief. Now she could concentrate on Ikot Obong and the Creek settlements.

Almost immediately she was asked by the High Commissioner to become Vice-President of the Native Court for the area, and so she became the first woman magistrate in the British Empire. He knew from the past that she would refuse payment, and proposed a nominal salary of one pound a year, with the balance to be used for her missionary work. With her uncanny understanding of the native psyche and fluent Efik – the language also of many Ibibios – she began to be in demand by other officials looking for help with their own problems. One described how, with rapier-like precision she settled in minutes what had taken him three days to get nowhere.

Being theoretically still on leave from Akpap, she was flouting authority by establishing herself at Ikot Obong, but was more concerned with 'dragging a great church behind her', to quote W P Livingstone, than observing protocol. In fact she was ready to separate herself if necessary, and use her full salary as Vice-President to support the family, for her missionary work was beginning to be subsidised by private donations. When recalled to Akpap, Mary categorically refused to go, knowing Janet Wright was returning from furlough and was willing to fill her place. The Calabar Mission Council backed down, aware of her huge following at home; nevertheless she was warned that in future she might suggest, but *it* would make the decisions.

She did go back to Akpap, but only to say farewell to her 'very dear people'. Their departure was remembered by Dan Slessor, six years old at the time:

> *It was a most pathetic morning; wailing rent the air, you cannot imagine a whole people so stricken and distressed; swarms of them came from distant villages with all sorts of presents including yams, plantains, goats, chickens and eggs … as the launch moved off … the great wail went up like thunder, men and women weeping. Ma stood on the upper deck, waving emotionally and as the launch turned the bend she collapsed into her chair.*

It was one of the most distressing moments of Mary's life. Her one consolation was knowing that Janet Wright had already proved her mettle at Akpap and would have Mina Amess, a promising new recruit, to assist her.

The Ibibios had been oppressed for centuries, and Mary described them thus:

> *They are the food and oil producers and they have been so numerous that they have been the happy hunting ground for slaves, and the down-trodden of Calabar and all the middle men tribes. They were bought for half the price of the Aros, and hence they are sulky, deceitful and in every sense inferior. They are neverthe-less the workers; alert, lithe, silent, they glide past everyone as quickly as they can, as if in fear. But they can be won ….*

She had already won their trust, and they had built accommodation and a church/school with remarkable speed. Her amazingly adaptable children again seemed to take the move in their stride; it was the price they paid for having a mother like Mary. But if their way of life was erratic, paradoxically it was also stable, for she loved all of them. And it was never dull. Travelling up the Enyong Creek one day, their journey was interrupted by the sudden appearance of a hippopotamus heading straight for them. Had she been alone, Mary would have been petrified, but she had her bairns to protect, which made the difference. Dan Slessor recorded the moment:

> *Her first concern, as usual, was not to create a fright or excitement among us, lest one might tumble overboard. Calmly she rose to her full height, oblivious of the tossing of the frail craft … and taking a long bamboo stick, she threw it with all her might and shouted out, 'Go away, you!' To the utter surprise of the paddlers, the hippo dipped, foamed and made away.*

The significance of this huge creature apparently obeying her wasn't lost on the paddlers, who in spreading the word added much to the legend of Akamba Ma.

Having established herself at Ikot Obong, Mary was presented with a bicycle by Charles Partridge. It was a great moment for her whole family who all fought to ride 'Enan Ukwak' (the iron cow) and, after a few shaky starts, soon she was speeding along roads as brand-new as her bicycle. 'Fancy an old woman like me on a cycle!' she said, admitting it had done her all the good in the world. Between the bicycle and government launches she was able to cover ground and water at a remarkable rate, and mud churches and schools were springing up everywhere. Later Partridge gave her a phonograph which they tried out together at an improvised service:

> *I spoke into the 'trumpet' the parable of the Prodigal and it was reproduced twice over in a trumpet tone. The audience was simply electrified. That parable has gone to be reproduced all over the Ibibio towns where our Administrator will be going on his civilising and governing tours. Is it not grand? ….*

Also grand was one particular evening at New Year when Janet Wright and Mina Amess came up from Akpap. Three surveyors at a nearby camp invited them to dinner, and Mary arrived in a dressing-gown, the nearest approach to formal wear she could muster. Despite corks being kept firmly in the bottles in deference to her, spirits were high, and she was in sparkling form.

Meanwhile an ordained minister, John Rankin, had volunteered to work at Arochuku, having gone with Mary and seen for himself its potential. Anxious for someone to take it over, she had offered to provide a decent mission house at her own expense. Whether or not her offer was accepted, it did stimulate action and Rankin was now in residence. In the interval, the Christian chief Okoyom had his carefully built church and whole village destroyed by flooding. Held responsible by his people for bringing disaster upon them through the destruction of their sacred ju-ju, he was in despair until Mary pointed out that God obviously wanted him to rebuild a better place on higher ground. The result was a model village, well ahead of its time, with a new church at its centre. It was called Obio Usiere, the Town of the Dawn.

But she was often fighting illness, and when unable to walk carried out her duties transported in a hammock by four boys. Her rheumatism made her irritable and she admitted to Charles Partridge that she was losing her temper too often in court. Increasingly he would become her father confessor, although many years her junior and a self-confessed 'pagan overlaid with a very thin veneer of Christianity'. He learned that she had boxed the ears of a lying, conniving chief one day, to everyone's amusement, and that another time, goaded beyond endurance by one unruly character, she had grabbed his umbrella and thumped him over the head with it.

Yet she consistently championed the cause of women. She railed against a system which gave them no status within the community, with wives simply the property of their husbands to exploit or dispose of at will. In a well-worn Bible, she even took St Paul to task in his rules regarding the subjection of women to husbands, scribbling indignantly in the margin: 'Na! na! Paul, laddie! This will no' do!' If abandoned, women were forced to prostitution to survive, and those unmarried, outside the protection of the law, were particularly vulnerable. She recommended that the wives of a man sentenced to lengthy imprisonment should, in accordance with past tradition, make 'friend' marriages in the interval to protect themselves and their children, a surprising commendation from a Victorian spinster of Mary's persuasion. But she was realistic enough to know it was better than the alternative. Hers was a court where women were seldom the losers.

Her ongoing crusade to remove the stigma attached to twins was having an effect, with a published government report of 1907 revealing that more mothers with twins were being accepted back into their families: 'The result is a sign of the civilising influence through the Court by that admirable lady, Miss Slessor.' However, abandoned women continued to be sheltered in her yard, and she became immersed in finding a scheme to ease their plight. Her idea for a women's settlement where they could be self-sufficient by growing their own food and selling the surplus was only the beginning, for they had other skills to be utilised. A site was located a few miles away at Use, and money was donated from Scotland for this purpose. But it never properly took off until later, for after its establishment a more urgent need took over.

Janet Wright left to get married and Mina Amess was assigned to assist Mary at Ikot Obong. Warned to go prepared, the newcomer brought her own domestic equipment, including a water filter, and Mary watched with wry amusement 16 bearers offloading all the paraphernalia, while Mina grew more embarrassed by the minute. But she was pleasantly surprised by the redoubtable Miss Slessor: 'Her originality, brightness and almost girlish spirit fascinated me .... One could not be long in her presence without enjoying a right hearty laugh.' And Mary, short-handed because Jean was in hospital with a 'female complaint', was relieved to have someone as 'sane and capable and helpful – she is always on the watch to see what is to be done ... a dear lassie'.

A bad outbreak of boils, diarrhoea and fever put Mary out of action, and the Itu doctor told her she must go home before she killed herself. This appeared to stimulate her recovery and before long she was off again. She acquired a hut on the site of the women's settlement at Use, and moved in with her family when two female agents from Duke Town were assigned to Ikot Obong. To her immense satisfaction, support from the Calabar Mission Council, slow in coming, was at last building up. However between cementing floors, visiting new outposts, and presiding over courts, she exhausted herself as usual and her fever returned. She later admitted to Partridge that this time she thought she would never walk again.

Finally she gave in to concerted pressure and agreed to go home. It would be her final visit. She took young Dan with her, leaving Jean in charge at Use, for Mina Amess was back in Akpap with an assistant of her own. Partridge had allayed Mary's fears for the safety of her 'big girls', promising to keep an eye on them during her absence.

With Dan and a fellow missionary, also going on furlough, to look after her, she was carried aboard the ship, where rest and good food helped her recovery. Soon she was walking again and ready to measure up to expectations back home. It was nine years since they had seen her, and her Scottish friends found her greatly changed in appearance, but still game for anything – except public speaking. Ladylike, she drove through Edinburgh streets in Miss Adam's carriage, and actually spent money (although conscience-stricken) on a grey silk suit which she said made her feel like a bride. She also went back to Dundee to the haunts of her youth and met old friends, revelling in hearing her Christian name again, an informality frowned upon in mission circles.

Yet despite the kindness showered upon them, the prospect of addressing meetings overshadowed her days. However release came in an unexpected way. Four months into her furlough she received word that Jean was misbehaving with a chief back home, and had she not been forced to honour three commitments, Mary would have been on the next boat. On her return, overwhelmed by relief on realising the rumour was without foundation, 'she was much too grateful to be angry'.

Chapter 12
The End of Her Journey

A GROUP from a large market town, Ikpe, 20 miles up a tribu tary of the Enyong Creek, arrived one day to remind Mary she had promised to come to them two years before and they had built a church in readiness for her. Their desire to abandon the old ways had resulted in their persecution, and although Ikpe was a considerable distance away and practically inaccessible by canoe during the dry season, she knew she must respond. She was free to do so now, having recently resigned from the Native Court after a serious disagreement with the current District Commissioner. Mistakenly believing he was in hospital, she had taken control over a matter outwith her remit, to which he had taken exception, but she admitted only to Partridge her sense of hurt when her resignation was accepted.

Meanwhile, her adopted children were growing up. Annie, steady and hard-working, had married an upstanding African trader, Akpan Inyang a Christian convert, and was living in Itu, and Mary's namesake – 'the child of wonder' who had survived being abandoned for a week in the bush as an infant – had followed her example. Her husband, from Lagos, was the handsome driver of the government motor car. He was also Christian and well educated. Her girls had matured quickly and she had encouraged them to marry young for their own protection, aware that her time was running out. Dan and Asuquo – a later family member – now attended the Hope Waddell Institute and two of her girls were at school in Duke Town, so her permanent household was reduced, although it was always open to change.

Dysentery and what she called 'the funniest illness I have ever had', put an end to her immediate plans. Whatever it was, the illness was serious enough for the government car to dispatch her at top speed to

Itu hospital and Dr Robertson, who looked after her 'just as he might have done to his own mother'. Afterwards the Macgregors took her back to Duke Town where she was persuaded to meet a woman journalist from the *London Morning Post* who was anxious to interview her. Sometimes Mary enjoyed her reputation as an eccentric, which had been enhanced recently after a missionary from Duke Town paid her a visit. The visitor had to be up early to catch the launch back the following morning, and had discovered that Mary didn't possess an alarm clock. Instead she captured a cockerel which she tied by one leg to her own bed. 'When we blow out out the lamp, he'll bide quiet till dawn,' she said. 'He aye does!' With such a name to protect, she now delved into the mission boxes for suitably eccentric clothing and this newspaper report was the outcome:

> *I am not given to admiring missionary enterprise. The enthusiasm which seems to many magnificent, seems to me but meddling in other people's business. But this missionary conquered me if she did not convert me. She was a woman close on sixty with a heavily lined face and a skin from which the freshness and bloom had long departed, but there was fire in her old eyes still, tired though they looked … Heaven knew who had dressed her. She wore a skimpy tweed skirt and a cheap nun's veiling blouse, and on her iron-grey hair was perched rakishly, a forlorn, broken picture-hat of faded green chiffon with a knot of bright red ribbon to give the bizarre touch of colour ….*

The piece ended with a quote from the High Commissioner:

> *She, Miss Slessor, can go where no white man can go. She can sway the people where we cannot sway them.*

Back at Use after 'five idle Sabbaths', Mary maintained she had fully recovered, and set off for Ikpe, accompanied by Martha Peacock, one of the two women missionaries now at Ikot Obong and the second Falkirk schoolgirl to end up in Calabar. Writing earlier to Partridge – who had been transferred to Lagos to her intense disappointment – she had extolled Martha's kindness and said, 'Her sane way of looking at things now that she has the right clue, are a great help to me'. At Ikpe they were greeted by women clad only in decorative coloured chalk patterns, but whose heads were covered by scarves. Recalling St Paul's strict rules regarding women's head-covering, Mary grinned at Martha and asked if she thought he had been there before them.

She would pay many visits to Ikpe. The Macgregors, worried about her health, found her proposal to itinerate between Use and Ikpe on a regular basis utterly foolhardy and decided to accompany her on one of her trips. On the eve of departure she was ill with fever, but after midnight had staggered up, determined to leave there and then. When they protested that she was too sick to travel, Jean said Ma was often like this. 'She just takes laudanum and lies down in the canoe and sleeps. By the end of the journey she is better. She has been doing it for months.' And sure enough, by the time they reached Ikpe Mary had recovered. So warm was their reception that she turned to them. 'You see? I'm honour bound to come.' Appalled by the filthy town and 'degraded' people, they nevertheless recognised they wouldn't budge her once her mind was set. Calabar Presbytery had found this out the hard way. Alexander Cruickshank, now the senior missionary, had earlier complained to Mr Wilkie, a friend of Mary's, that Miss Slessor had been particularly difficult at a Presbytery meeting, whereupon Wilkie reminded him that she had been very ill. 'Aye,' replied Cruickshank dryly, 'and it's been a lang illness!'

Partridge had heard nothing from her for several weeks, and as the ball was usually in his court regarding letter-writing, he became alarmed and sent her a telegram. Her reply was scarcely legible:

Very dear old friend,
I only got your telegram last week .... I went very ill with at least a hundred boils over my head .... I lay down, or stretched across is nearer the thing, Mrs Wilkie's bed and for a whole month was in a prolonged agony of pain. The boils came in shoals ... until you would not have recognised me ... and whenever I got over one operation of having the cores pressed out, another began, and I cried like a

child … when I was not shrieking …. I could not read because my eyelids were full and letters were left unopened …. Poor hair! Poor head! It is as bald as a sixpence all over the back …. The few hairs left at the front are like those of a doll's head put on with bad glue.

Horrified, Partridge apparently questioned if it was all worthwhile and begged her to go home to Scotland, which provoked this response:

I love my Master and I will not go out from Him, and I do believe that I am doing Ikpe and Use good by giving them that which takes away the hunger of the spirit, and gives them a definite tangible Helper and hope and life. So there!!!

She was back in Ikpe with 50 sheets of corrugated iron within weeks to build a permanent roof over her head, and spurred two hundred men into clearing bushland for an outstation. Unfortunately, when a mission representative came to sanction the undertaking, he declared it was the unhealthiest spot he had ever visited and no missionary in their right mind would go there. Except Mary. Her pioneering spirit was recharged and the lack of the British presence which had latterly smoothed her path added an edge to the situation. One day after she waded in to stop bloodshed in the market place, an old chief came up to thank her. 'He held out both his hands for mine, which I gladly gave to him …. It is a real life I am living now, not all preaching and holding meetings ….' Again she was rescuing twins, and through bantering and coaxing succeeded in vaccinating everyone during a smallpox scare when government agents who had been allocated the job were chased off.

Having established herself, she was able to return frequently to Use and latterly would have the benefit of a new road and a government car to assist her most of the way. By mail order she selected a Cape cart (a basket chair on wheels) which Wellington Street Church in Glasgow donated, and discarded the hammock which had made her feel like a brute 'to be lying there while four boys sweated like beasts of burden'.

When Dr Robertson went on furlough, a newcomer, Dr Hitchcock, arrived at Itu to take his place. Mary had met her match in Hitchcock and they battled furiously. In a letter home he described his patient:

Without exaggeration here is a name to conjure with. Her influence is felt over hundreds of square miles. She had been ill before we came into collision. She wanted to go to some outlandish place (Ikpe) fifteen hours by canoe far from any white man .... I only stopped her by threatening to close all work at Itu and to follow her. This was effectual and since then she has been amenable. She has really been very ill – it is her heart – and I am obliged to see her every day .... She compels admiration, she is utterly heroic. She has a brilliant mind, incredibly keen. I am glad to say that she is improving but she is so frightfully headstrong. She will not rest and resting is the one thing which is essential ....

Mary wrote to Partridge that Hitchcock was a rare man, a rare Christian and a rare doctor, and she was vexed at vexing him. James Macgregor recorded one of their exchanges:

'You are hopelessly undernourished,' said Hitchcock. 'You must eat meat.'
'I am not a meat eater,' said Mary. 'Why did you send me that cooked chicken?'
'Because it could not get here by itself. And you will eat it!'

At Ikpe she was particularly undernourished, although she made sure the children fared better. She wrote, 'It is very difficult to get money brought from Calabar and then the people won't take English money when it comes.' (The usual currency was copper rods.) When her chickens were lost or stolen she was forced to send Alice to the market with any saleable goods she could muster to raise enough to buy yams and a few small fish. Without the Africans who were generous with gifts of food, and provisions from the mission boxes – especially tea, her one addiction (apart from toffee) – often she would have starved. However she had utter confidence in God's providence.

The newly acquired Cape cart gave her a new lease of life and she postponed her furlough, but on the insistence of her doctor and a generous Scottish benefactor, finally agreed to go to the Canaries with Jean. A favourite of Mary's, Agnes Young, who had also come to Calabar through her influence, helped them to become 'wiselike and decent' enough to face a month in a posh hotel, where Mary promised to wear her new wardrobe. She and Jean were equally apprehensive, but were treated with great kindness throughout. For Mary, free from all commitments, it was the most wonderful holiday she ever had. Back at Duke Town, and more amenable because of improved health, she attended a reception at the express invitation of the Governor-General of all Nigeria, Sir Frederick Lugard, who said he was proud to shake her hand. His brother Edward wrote in his diary that day:

> *Reading her life story – as I recently had occasion to do in drafting a dispatch to the Secretary of State asking for H.M.'s bestowal of some recognition of her great service ... a great lump rises in one's throat. The long years of not quiet, but fierce devotion – for they say she is a tornado – unrecognised, and without hope of, or desire for, recognition.*

Meanwhile, Mary was persuaded to have a complete medical check-up and was told if she took proper care she would be good for some time yet. She fully intended to follow the advice and returned to Use laden with medicine and even a water filter and mosquito net. However these were often left behind with her good intentions on setting out for Ikpe – where she needed them most.

The year 1913 was marked by two significant events. Invited back to Akpap for the opening of a new church, Mary was given a rapturous welcome after eight years' absence. Her reunion with her 'dear friend and almost sister' Ma Eme – as heathen as ever – was mutually joyful and it was obvious that Mary's successor, Mina Amess, was doing a good job. Again there was an emotional farewell from her people – for they would always remain her people – and again the tears streamed down her face.

Soon afterwards she was summoned to Duke Town to receive the honour recommended by Sir Frederick Lugard and she was now an Honorary Associate of the Order of St John of Jerusalem. To her consternation her award, a silver Maltese Cross (now displayed in the McManus Galleries, Dundee) had been presented publicly but, dressed reasonably neatly in a borrowed straw hat and a Canaries dress from which her plimsolls peeped beneath, she emphasised that she was accepting the honour on behalf of the whole missionary community, and made light of her own efforts. 'If I have done anything in my life it has been easy, because the Master has gone before.' For days she was the focus of commemorative events, and couldn't wait to escape. 'I shall never be able to look the world in the face again until all this blarney and publicity is over.'

Returning to Ikpe, her new objective was reputedly dangerous territory beyond Odoro Ikpe, six miles away, where she attempted without proper assistance to turn an abandoned government building into a mission base. Unable to rest until she had won over chiefs entrenched in the old ways, she squandered her health yet again. She was constantly driven by fear that there would be none to succeed her:

> *We are lower in numbers in Calabar than ever ... surely there is something far wrong with our Church .... We have really no workers to meet all this opened country ... and our Church, to be honest, should stand back and give it to someone else ... But oh! I cannot think of that ....*

Earlier, Partridge had sent her a replacement bicycle, but she could no longer ride it and confessed she was 'lame, feeble and foolish; the wrinkles are wonderful – no concertina is so wonderfully folded and convoluted. I'm a wee, wee wifie, very little buikit [built] but I grip on well nonetheless'. However, surviving diaries tell a story of increasing illness, hardship and loneliness. But still she could write:

> *Mine has been such a joyous service .... God has been good to me .... I cannot thank him enough for the honour He conferred on me when He sent me to the Dark Continent.*

And to another:

Give up your whole being to create music everywhere, in the light places, and in the dark places, and your life will make melody.

Back at Use after more illness, Mary knew she had finally run her course. When Dan returned at Christmas he wept at her appearance, her gauntness accentuated by her having stopped wearing her dentures. Her girls, gentle and caring, along with Martha, and Beatrice Welsh who had taken over an outstation nearby – of whom Mary said 'she fits mission life like a glove' – all rallied round as she struggled on. Partridge's letters had almost ceased, and she confessed his defection had taken much zest from life. Yet he continued to send plum puddings each Christmas and kept all her letters. In her final one she wrote:

My dear old friend,
The plum puddings have just come ... and the whole lot of us are to have one tonight which has caused great excitement and all are jumping about like crazy things .... Whitie is away to the village to tell Annie .... If I can hold out till March I shall probably take a trip to Scotland or at least to [Grand] Canary ....

She still insisted on being carried to church to take the services and continued to take pleasure in her children and grandchildren. On 2 January she wrote:

Annie's wee girlie (Susie) is the sweetest pet, and imitates everything and everybody. She runs about in church, and will point to me during the service and call to me, yet I CAN'T say don't bring her. There should be room in our Father's House for even the babies.

Sadly the trip to Scotland or the Canaries was not to be, for Mary collapsed again shortly afterwards and lingered semi-conscious for several days. She died on 13 January 1915, aged 67, surrounded by the family she loved and who loved her. Martha Peacock was beside her when she prayed in the Efik which came so naturally: 'Abasi, sana mi yak' (O God, release me), before she quietly slipped away.

Epilogue

THE mission launch took Mary downriver for the last time, where her coffin lay on board until morning. The bush telegraph had conveyed the sad news, and throughout the night canoes assembled bearing representatives from every tribe whose lives had touched hers. Immediately he heard the news, the Governor-General sent the mission secretary a telegraph: 'It is with the deepest regret that I learn of the death of Miss Slessor. Her death is a great loss to Nigeria.'

Flags flew at half-mast as the community mourned, and when the funeral procession moved to the cemetery, the road was lined by troops, missionaries, schoolchildren and students from the Hope Waddell Institute. Most impressive of all was the sight of hundreds of Africans, earlier prostrate with grief, who now in a supreme effort of self-control contained their sorrow and honoured Eka Kpukpro Owo (the Mother of the Peoples) with dignity, their last magnificent way of showing their love and respect. After the funeral a rose grown from a slip by Mary at Use, from a bouquet she was given after receiving her Maltese Cross, was planted and took root, which would surely have pleased her.

Tributes poured in from every part, and although richly deserved one wonders what Mary would have made of the 'blarney and publicity' this time. Those who knew her well said it wasn't 'our Mary', and perhaps James Macgregor described her best: 'Mary Slessor was a whirlwind and an earthquake, and a fire and a still small voice, all in one.'

Maggie and Alice were given a home with Martha Peacock, while Whitie, the last girl to join Mary's family, remained with Jean, an able evangelist who continued Mary's work at Use but died in an influenza epidemic in 1918. After his training, Dan found work with the Nigerian Forestry Commission, later becoming a journalist, and Asuquo went off to sea. What eventually happened to Mary's three unmarried girls is unknown.

Agnes Young – now Arnot – one of Mary's favourites, returned to Calabar after her husband died, and became the first Mary Slessor Memorial Missionary to carry on her work, moving the women's settlement to Arochuku and expanding it. She also established several outstations around Ikpe. Mary's other special girls, Martha Peacock, Mina Amess and Beatrice Welsh continued and consolidated the work she had begun, proving the accuracy of her assessment of them. On 28 September 1923 a magnificent memorial window to her memory was unveiled in Dundee's Museum and Art Galleries – now the McManus Galleries – and when a Mary Slessor Corner was opened there on 11 September 1953 by the Moderator of the Church of Scotland, Agnes Arnot was an honoured guest.

Back at Use, a simple cairn by the roadside marks the place where Mary died, an appropriate memorial for one to whom outward show meant little. On a hillside above Duke Town – now incorporated into the bustling town of Calabar, the principal town of the Calabar region – there stands a larger and more imposing monument, a huge cross of Aberdeen granite gifted by the people of Scotland, of which Charles Ovens said at the time:'It'll tak mair than that tae hold doon oor Mary!'

Some years later in the Mary Slessor Hospital at Itu, when R M McDonald finished giving a lantern lecture, he was asked by an old chief for the white sheet he had used as a screen. 'Why?' asked McDonald, and learned it was because Mary's likeness had been imposed on it. 'She was my friend,' the old man said simply, 'and I like that face too well.'

Bibliography

AJAYI, J F A: *Christian Missions in Nigeria 1841-91: the Making of a New Elite* (London 1965).

BUCHAN, James: *The Expendable Mary Slessor* (Saint Andrew Press, Edinburgh 1980).

BUCHAN, James: *Peacemaker of Calabar: The Story of Mary Slessor* (Religious and Moral Education Press, Exeter 1984).

CHRISTIAN, Carol and Gladys PLUMMER: *God and One Redhead: Mary Slessor of Calabar* (Hodder and Stoughton, London 1970).

CHURCH of SCOTLAND OVERSEAS COUNCIL: *Mary Slessor of Calabar* (Church of Scotland Overseas Council, Edinburgh 1978).

DAVIDSON, Thomas M: *The Mary Slessor Window: Descriptive Notes and Short Biography* (Dundee 1924).

DIKE, Onwuka: *Trade and Politics in the Niger Delta 1830-1885* (Oxford 1956).

FORDE, Darryl: *Efik Traders in Old Calabar* (Oxford 1956).

GOLDIE, Hugh: *Calabar and its Mission* (Edinburgh 1890).

GOLDIE, Hugh: *Memorials of King Eyo VII* (Church of Scotland pamphlet, National Library of Scotland).

HOGG, Jessie: *The Story of the Calabar Mission* (1902).

KINGSLEY, Mary: *Travels in West Africa* (London 1897).

LIVINGSTONE, W P: *Mary Slessor of Calabar: Pioneer Missionary* (Hodder and Stoughton, London 1915).

LIVINGSTONE, W P: *Mary Slessor the White Queen* (Hodder and Stoughton, London 1933).

LUKE, James: *Pioneering in Mary Slessor's Country* (Epworth Press, London 1929).

McFARLAN, Donald: *Calabar* (London 1963).

McFARLAN, Donald: *White Queen: the Story of Mary Slessor* (Lutterworth Press, London 1955).

Minutes of United Presbyterian Foreign Missions' Board 1880 and 1885 (Edinburgh: National Library of Scotland).

Missionary Record – United Presbyterian Church Magazine (Edinburgh: National Library of Scotland).

O'BRIEN, Brian: *She had a Magic: the Story of Mary Slessor* (Jonathan Cape, London 1958).

PERHAM, Margery: *Lugard: The Years of Authority* (London 1960).

SLESSOR, Daniel McArthur: *Reminiscences of Miss Mary Slessor* (Dundee: Local Studies Department of Central Library).

SLESSOR, Mary: Photocopies of letters (Dundee: Local Studies Department of Central Library, City Archives, Arts and Heritage Department of McManus Galleries).

SLESSOR Mary: *Letters to Charles Partridge* (Dundee: Local Studies Department of Central Library) at **www.dundeecity.gov.uk**

Places to Visit

G O to the McManus Galleries, Albert Square, Dundee, if only for the Mary Slessor window on the ground floor. Choose a sunny day for spectacular effect.

Dundee Central Library has a number of books and papers relating to Mary Slessor in its local history section (on the first floor of the Wellgate Shopping Centre, off the Cowgate).

You can also visit the Wishart Church in St Roque's Lane, Dundee. Look out for the plaque commemorating Mary Slessor above Wishart Pend. There is a brass plaque to the left on a pillar between two shops.

Continuing up St Roque's Lane, on Princess Street to the right is the site of Baxter's, a spinning mill erected in 1850 where Mary worked from the age of eleven. The mill has since been converted into residential flats but the frontage remains.

Postscript

WHILE writing this book I tried without success to track down information regarding the descendants of Mary Slessor's adopted family and it was only on the verge of going to print that the breakthrough finally came. The source was unexpected – the January 2001 issue of the Church of Scotland's magazine *Life & Work*. On the cover of was a picture of a young Nigerian, with the caption: 'Mary Slessor's Living Legacy.' This was Francis Ita Udom, the great grandson of Annie, one of Mary's adopted children. On reading the covering article, my excitement grew as I realised that Francis was actually living in Glasgow, only an hour's journey from my home. Amazingly, two days later, we were sharing a meal together.

When we met on a bitterly cold evening, with his face almost hidden by a snug-fitting woollen hat, it seemed that only his eyes were visible, until he gave a smile to melt the stoniest of hearts. His first January in Scotland was proving a testing time; a stark contrast to the tropical climate of home.

Sponsored by Glasgow-based Denholm Ship Management on behalf of Nigerian Liquified Natural Gas Co (NLNG) – 23 year-old Francis is presently on a three-year course studying marine engineering at Glasgow's College of Nautical Studies. He has integrated well into Glasgow life and brought his own musical talent into its Philharmonic Male Voice Choir. However he was profoundly shaken recently when he came across a Scottish Clydesdale £10 banknote which showed a map of his own village in Nigeria on the back. On the other side there was a portrait of Mary Slessor, who had rescued and adopted his great grandmother Annie, many years before. It was the first indication he had of being in Mary's homeland, for despite having known of the relationship between Annie and Mary through his grandmother Susie – of whom Mary was very fond – he had never realised that his adoptive great great grandmother was Scottish.

Educated in the Presbyterian Church of Nigeria School, Francis had sought out Presbyterian churches on his arrival in Glasgow and was befriended by Mrs Morris, wife of the minister of the Cathedral, to whom he confided his connection with Mary Slessor. Through her her, he met Rev S MacQuarrie, who contacted *Life & Work*. Since then, Francis has been the focus of media attention, even being interviewed by a film company which already had a major film on Mary's life under-way. (Awareness that this film was in the pipeline had initially prompted this book, along with the realisation that few of today's generation who noticed Mary's likeness on a banknote, replacing that of David Livingstone, would appreciate its significance – to honour one of the most remarkable Scotswomen of any generation.)

Francis is immensely proud of his connection with Mary and she would have been equally proud of him. His father Ignatius is a civil servant with the Forestry Department in Nigeria and is a practising Catholic in a predominantly Catholic area. His mother Emilia is also employed in related work, the Ministry of Agriculture, and like most of the family is Presbyterian. They all recognise the importance of education, with Francis' brother Ignatius at Calabar University and Godwin about to enter Uyo University in Ibibio. His elder sister, another Susie, is already there, while the second youngest, Elizabeth, is at a convent school. The baby of the family, who carries the proud name of Mary Slessor, is at a local school.

In the 1940s Francis' grandparents moved from Ikot Nseyen in Ibibio to Use Ikot Oku, 30 miles away. Their son – Francis' father Ignatius – married a local girl, Emilia, the grand-daughter of Mary's adopted daughter, Annie. Their home in Use is only a stone's throw away from Mary Slessor's memorial cairn which Emilia still visits daily. It is an act of remembrance and thanksgiving for the remarkable woman without whom neither she, Francis nor any of Annie's other descendants would ever have been born.